Ruthann Knechel Johansen

COMING TOGETHER

male and female in a renamed garden

THE BRETHREN PRESS

The poem "housewife," which appears on page 112, is reprinted from *All My Pretty Ones,* by Anne Sexton, copyright 1961, 1962 by Anne Sexton and published by Houghton Mifflin Company. Used by permission.

Library of Congress Cataloging in Publication Data

Johansen, Ruthann Knechel
   Coming together.

   Bibliography: p.
   1. Women in Christianity. 2. Sex role.
3. Sex discrimination against women. 4. Sex
(Theology) I. Title.
BV639.W7J64   261.8'34'1   77-6301
ISBN 0-87178-156-5

for the little people

The wolf also shall dwell with the lamb, and the leopard shall lie down with the kid; and the calf and the young lion and the fatling together; and a little child shall lead them.

Isaiah 11:6

CONTENTS

INTRODUCTION

My initiation into adulthood occurred simultaneously with the social and political ferment that characterized the 1960s. The civil rights movement, accompanied by the Vietnam War and an awakening liberation consciousness of Third World people and of women, brought me into a thorny encounter with the contemporary Christian church. I understood the cries for liberation first as a woman. The general indifference of many Christian congregations to the immorality and illegality of the war, to the continuing oppression of racial minorities, and to the imperialism of wealthy nations against poorer ones compelled me to examine the oppression I know first hand as a woman and which I cannot separate from other forms of oppression.

Now a decade later, liberation pleas are still abroad in the world: The disenfranchised South Africans seek justice against violence; the poor in Pakistan starve or live malnourished lives while wealthy Americans consume more than half of the world's resources; polluted life-sources threaten animal, plant, and human existence; billions of dollars for defense machinery are spent by so-called super powers as farmers in Bangladesh slowly learn how to use their soil more productively. Meanwhile, thousands and thousands of Americans browse in bookstores to examine the writings of various self-fulfillment cults. What shall we choose: transcendental meditation or *The Total Woman?* We ask what leaves us empty amidst our plenty? The church, too, gropes in the search, wondering what God requires. Is salvation a personal, spiritual experience of grace? Or does salvation call us into a new obedience that Jesus described for himself:

> The Spirit of the Lord is upon me,
> because he has anointed me to preach good news to the poor.
> He has sent me to proclaim release to the captives
> and recovering of sight to the blind,
> to set at liberty those who are oppressed,
> to proclaim the acceptable year of the Lord.
>
> (Luke 4:18-19; see also Isaiah 61:1)

I have pursued my thorny encounter with the church because I believe that liberation/salvation is at the heart of the Christian message. Because I felt the liberation needs of women most closely related to my skin, I began to search within and with other women for explanations of the pervasive disrespect for life I found revealed in the ridicule of the women's movement, in the defense of the Vietnam War, in the mistrust of black, Indian, or Hispanic-Americans, and in ignorance of other large parts of the globe.

The result of that search is this book. It is about the impact of institutional religion on women in American society; it is written for women and men reared within the influence of the Christian church, particularly American Protestants. The book has two purposes. The first is to analyze the participation of the church in the oppression of woman and in the age-old alienation of woman from man, of human beings from nature, and, ultimately, of people from God. The second purpose is to suggest ways in which liberation must mean reunion: the reuniting of woman and man, of human beings and nature, of human beings with the divine,

Though I am indebted to fine scholars, particularly biblical scholars, historians, and philosophers, for their impact on this book directly and indirectly, the book is experiential and analytical rather than scholarly. In every way these pages are foremost my personal effort as a woman to give some form to the questioning, the loneliness, the bondage that many people, inside and outside the church, are experiencing.

The book pleads for consideration of the effects of our world views (how we see and think about the world) on our private lives and the practices of our culture. It differs from many of the books considering the liberation of women in that it assumes that liberation is impossible without reunion; therefore, it (1) criticizes the church for participating in the oppressive practices of the culture toward women; (2) ignores the more common idea that separation of women from men is the most direct route to liberation; (3) rejects the attempts by women to gain power over men as a road to liberation; and (4) asserts that liberation is realized as one loses his or her life in the creation of new life and a new order around one.

Some assumptions which underlie my work should be explicit. I think that Western religious belief may be the unsound foundation upon which our isolated identities and our fragmented relationships to the world are built. Whether or not we personally espouse orthodox religious beliefs about the nature of the divine and of humanity, we do not escape the pervasive influence on the total culture of Western religious doctrine. A common view of the divine for the Western mind is God as father, separate from the self and beyond this world. This anthropomorphic, masculine God is sometimes loving, sometimes judging, sometimes wrathful, and sometimes apparently indifferent. But "He" is always "out there" beyond the intimate experiences of earth.

For many persons, this separate God in perfection and omnipotence exists in tension with human beings. "He" stands over-against creation. One learns about such a God little by little by conforming to "His" ways; one may be taught that relationship with God is assured only through decision to deny oneself and to seek the nebulous will of God outside one's own being and experience in a spiritual state that is cut off from the flesh and the earth. People who hold such an understanding of God will probably view human beings as fallen angels and nature as the handiwork of a *deus ex machina.*[1]

Symptoms of alienation from the world of nature and from each other that derive from such religious outlooks are plentiful. Science teaches us to study nature as a collection of phenomena to be observed, analyzed, categorized; we believe that human survival depends in large part on the human capacity to understand objectively and to have dominion over the natural world.

Our human relationships are conducted and studied in similar ways and reflect our assumptions about the separation of human beings from God. We have been taught that successful separation of the child from a mothering person is essential for the psychological health of the child. The kind of separation many young people experience turns into competitive individualism and isolation which foster mistrust and disunity among people. Broken ties with a primary group, such as one can find in cultures where the extended family still functions, lead not finally to health and wholeness but to alienation. Consequently, until the time of death many separated individuals yearn for intimacy.

By contrast, wherever a sense of unity binds individuals, unequal, competitive relationships are improbable. Some families reveal this kind of unity, particularly when the life of the total group is dependent upon the beings, as well as the physical efforts, of each person. Because each one knows the necessity of interdependence for the life of the whole, unity and equality prevail over separateness and inequality. When unity is broken, when mutual interdependence is ignored, persons are taken for granted, manipulated, and their needs forgotten.

The possibility for either disintegration or union lies within each person. When you feel whole, that is, when you know yourself to be capable of thinking, ordering your own life, and of feeling and acting, you do not belittle the ideas of others, reject the feelings of others, or sabotage the work of others. Instead you are more likely to relate yourself to others in a spirit of cooperation or unity. If you learn to fear or reject yourself, you will be incapable of loving cooperation.

Oppressive practices toward fellow human beings grow from personal disintegration and interpersonal separation. The troublesome paradox for Western culture is that while it is the wealthiest, most highly industrialized, and most educated of all contemporary cultures, it also has been oppressive for large groups of people domestically and globally. Are wealth, industrialization, and power—by-products of education—necessarily the results of disintegration and separation? Will oppression cease when integration and reunion occur?

One of the most influential contributors to a Western separatist, fragmentary, and patriarchal world view has been the Christian church, despite its assumed contributions to civilization. Although reunion (described most often as reconciliation in the New Testament) seems to be a central motif of Jesus's earthly ministry, the church institutionally has often participated in human oppression. One can see the church's tragic acquiescence in oppression in the perennial human-technological domination of nature, in the separation of individuals from themselves, and in the so-called battle between the sexes. Other more institutionalized forms of oppression such as slavery and imperialism, both blessed at times in history by the church, may be said to spring from these primal separations prophesied, as it were, in the Genesis story of the fall.

Because of my persistent conviction that within each soul there lies unique humanity and divinity to be experienced and expressed in its own fashion and time, this book could not become narrowly prescriptive but instead must be open, probing, and consciousness-expanding. The goal of the book is communion: reunion of the self with the universe, with other human beings, and with the divine. If the book in any way facilitates an awakening of unique self-hood as part of "a seamless unity of nature,"[2] then a revolution of love that could liberate oppressor and oppressed moves closer to our experience. In such a revolution our fallen garden may be renamed for wholeness and become holy.

Chapter 1.

LIBERATION: WHERE IS
THE CHRISTIAN CHURCH?

In worldly affairs you may accept emancipation—and before God there is neither man nor woman—but in the church's life and worship it is not so.—Krister Stendhal

Women spend many hours performing Good Samaritan acts in the name of the church. Probably no other volunteer group or agency depends on the regular services of women as much as does the church. What have women learned from the church about themselves? What do they experience within the Christian fellowship?

My grandmother, I suspect, was a typical turn-of-the-century woman who placed the church at the center of her own and her family's life. She studied the Bible seriously; for a rural Pennsylvania woman with a heavy round of farm-associated duties, she read and thought eagerly. Her home was a veritable guest-house for itinerant preachers, and she fed any wayfarer as well as her family and friends. She was a tolerant woman who spoke for those whom others often were quick to reject. Yet she was not considered the church leader that my grandfather was. A month before her death, which she sensed was imminent, she spoke to me about her deep feelings of unworthiness and the fear that she had failed at that which she had tried so faithfully—to be a

Christlike person. Who or what is responsible for this kind of distress in women of all ages?

Though women for centuries have felt some confusion about their relationship to the Christian church, not unlike my grandmother's experience, the majority of them have accepted their ambiguous position in the church's life and have internalized the definitions of their nature and the prescriptions for their behavior that have come through the voices of the patriarchy past and present. At the 1854 Woman's Rights Convention a small group of women charged the church with denying women full personhood and misinterpreting the message of Jesus. Charges of this kind did not reach the ears and minds of most people in the church. At that meeting Hannah Tracy Cutler "showed that man and woman were a simultaneous creation, with equal power and glory on their heads . . . "[1] and Lucretia Mott said, "It is not Christianity, but priestcraft that has subjected woman as we find her. . . . "[2] Today Cutler and Mott could say the same words in many American churches and still be unheard.

What motivated Cutler and Mott in the past and women in the present who are beginning to sense a need for their own and others' liberation is a deep conviction that at the heart of Jesus' being and teaching was the potential experience of liberation or salvation. Because of their strong faith in the message of liberation and their awareness of the discrepancy between that message and church doctrine and practice, women are asking themselves and the church: How have we become who we are in the eyes of others and in our own eyes; are we second class, inferior, subject to men, wearing the alternating masks of temptress and virgin mother?

The language customs of the culture and of the church give us clues to why women feel excluded from full participation. Similarly, an examination of the church's liturgies, its attitudes toward leadership, its sacraments such as marriage, its education, and its service provides a basis on which to confront the question: Is the church genuinely a liberator of human beings in the spirit of Christ?

The language of our culture shapes our perceptions of reality, psycholinguists have observed for years, but we fail to grasp the extent to which language traditions serve our stereotypes. We also fail to understand that nearly everything we ever learn comes through our symbols and our language. Andrew Greeley writes that "man is a symbol-creating animal. He orders and interprets his reality by his symbols, and he uses the symbols to reconstruct that reality."[3] In this passage Greeley does more than just alert us to the function of symbols. His own use of language excludes half of the human family and perpetuates the notion of male dominance.

Though most readers of Greeley's words would have assumed through a long history of male-oriented language that he is using *man* in the inclusive sense, some thoughtful people today are asking what effect on our reality, our beliefs about male and female, such malist language has. In a patriarchy women are usually unrecognized in the symbols or symbol-making process. When the language makes them invisible by referring to humanity and its projects in predominantly male terms, the effect of such language is to perpetuate the general social exclusion of women.

In English it is considered accurate to use the masculine pronoun *he* when the sex of the person spoken about is undefined. In some other languages such custom is strange indeed. We have no inclusive term which covers both female and male in the singular form; in the plural, of course, we can use *we* or *they.* In French or German, for example, separate, indefinite pronouns are available when the sex of a person is unknown or irrelevant. The French word *son* means one and can apply to either female or male when the speaker is unclear about the specific sex involved. The German equivalent of *son* is the pronoun *man.* If a speaker tells about a person going, she or he would use the following forms:

Er geht, translated he goes;
Sie geht, translated she goes;
Man geht, translated one goes;
Es geht, translated it goes.

When talking about humanity again in English we commonly use *man* (in what we call the generic sense) or *mankind*. Because the word *humanity* has no specific sexual overtones, it could be used more accurately and inclusively of both men and women to describe male and female human beings in much the way that *'adham* was used in Genesis. In Hebrew *'adham* means man in the generic sense; therefore, in Genesis 2 when God created *'adham* he was a non-sexual or an androgynous being. When God created woman a different term *(ish)* is applied to *'adham*. *Ish* and *ishshah* (man and woman) are now differentiated as sexual beings, complementary of one another. In German the word *Mensch* refers to people or to humanity. A different word, *Mann*, means man. Instead of using the word *Mann* to stand for people, the Germans may more likely use *Mensch*, a separate word not connected directly with the term for biological man.

English and German translations of two passages of scripture may illustrate the difference in meaning. First from the Psalms: "What is man, that thou art mindful of him? And the son of man, that thou visitest him?" (Psalm 8:4, KJV). In German the translation is: *"Was ist der mensch, dass du seiner gedenkest, und des Menschen Kind, dass du dich seiner annimmst?"* Does the inclusive term *Mensch* expand the meaning of the Psalm?

The second example is from 1 Corinthians 13:1 (KJV):

> Though I speak with the tongues of men and of angels, and have not charity, I am become as sounding brass, or a tinkling cymbal.

And in German we find:

> *Wenn ich mit Menschen= und mit Engelzungen redete, und hätte der Lube nicht, so ware ich ein tonendes Erz, oder eine klingende Schelle.*

What effects might the simple substitution of a word like *humanity* for *man* have on the minds of women as well as on the attitudes of men?

In their excellent article on language, "One Small Step for Genkind," Casey Miller and Kate Swift report that

One of the most surprising challenges to our male-dominated culture is coming from within organized religion, where the issues are being stated, in part, by confronting the implications of traditional language.[4]

The language of Christian liturgy is very heavily filled with male symbolism. God, who is not a person but whose Hebrew name is Yahweh (YHWH), derived from the verbal root meaning *to be* or *to exist,* is addressed commonly with a male name and pronoun. The Scriptures, understandably so because they were framed in patriarchies not unlike our own, have primarily male terms even when the referents are not sexually or exclusively male. There seems to be a

connection between increasingly outmoded theological language and the accelerating number of women (and men) who are dropping out of organized religion, both Jewish and Christian. For language, including pronouns, can be used to construct a reality that simply mirrors society's assumptions. To women who are committed to the reality of religious faith, the effect is doubly painful. Professor Harvey Cox . . . stated the issue directly: The women, he said, were raising the basic theological question of whether God is more adequately thought of in personal or suprapersonal terms.[5]

Our creeds, our hymns, and our prayers petition God, the father; they call for men of God to rise up, for God to send us men, and for us all to fold to our hearts our brothers. To judge as petty a concern about the effect, on our perceptions of reality and particularly on our self-concepts, of malist language in the church is to reject the thousands of ways we permit language to control our thoughts and behavior in daily routine.

Does it actually make a difference to a woman if she thinks of God as a father? To some churchwomen it makes a significant difference. If human fathers are upheld in male-dominated societies as authoritarian disciplinarians, it seems difficult for some to approach with complete openness a God who is carved in a dominating human image. Making God either male or female is an absurd prescription. Can there be more honest, more precise ways of talking about God? Does a concept of God the father, God the mother, God the sister and brother, God as spirit, God as the essence of being and acting, God not a person but inclusively personal or suprapersonal, God in nature, God in and of all life—do these concepts not expand one's feelings of relationship with God?

Being a skeptic several years ago about the concern of male-oriented language in church liturgy, I set out to experiment with myself. When the words of hymns were male I tried, at first mentally and then vocally, to substitute either an inclusive term (such as human) or a female term. The song entitled "I See a New Day Coming," currently popular in many circles, contains the following refrain:

> I see a new day coming,
> A time when men are free,
> And they shall be his people,
> And they will walk with Him.[6]

Now I knew well that men in this refrain is supposed to refer to all persons, but as I sang with the following word substitutions I felt that I had come closer not only to the intent of the song but also to the heart of the Christian gospel:

> I see a new day coming,
> A time when *we* are free,
> And *we* shall be his people
> And *we* will walk with him.

This makes the song both male and female. And more importantly it demands personal involvement to sing it because of the pronoun *we* rather than *they*.

The voices rising within the church against malist language may, we can hope, lead to two conclusions. First, we may acknowledge what Elizabeth Farians, a Roman Catholic theologian, asserts: " . . . the bad theology of an over-masculinized church continues to be one of the root causes of women's oppression."[7] Second, we may be personally encouraged to join the too-small group of people who are actively urging a change in some of our terms. The change suggestion that Miller and Swift make, because they believe it would greatly expand our awareness of the oppressiveness of traditional language and because it would be more just to all human beings, is to use the word *gen* (as in genesis or generic) instead of mankind when referring to both sexes of people. Their defense of their term follows:

> Like the words deer and bison, gen would be both plural and singular. Like progenitor, progeny, and generation, it would convey continuity. Gen would express the warmth and generalized sexuality of generous, gentle, and genuine; the specific sexuality of genital and genetic. In the new family of gen, girls and boys would grow to genhood, and to speak of genkind would be to include all the people of the earth.[8]

If one feels resistant to such a change, she or he can wisely use the existing pronouns more accurately; and one can use both female and male pronouns when addressing both sexes.

In the West and within the Christian church we tend to equate hierarchical order with logical order. We have assumed for generations that because "the head of every man is Christ, [and] the head of a woman is her husband . . . " (1 Corinthians 11:3), men should lead in the religious life of the church. Therefore historically many people have accepted, as designed by God's natural, hierarchical order, the headship of man next to the headship of God. Christians have taught that Paul bore testimony to the virtue of male leadership in the sacred community in 1 Corinthians 14:33b-36. New Testament scholars, like Robin Scroggs, now view that quotation as post-Pauline because it is totally inconsistent with his opinion voiced in 1 Corinthians 11:2-16. The grip on the church fathers of the 1 Corinthians 14:33b-36 passage is still very strong; and for women it is merely one more evidence of their subordinate position as creations of a God, interpreted by male theologians to exist in the image of man.

Though several Protestant denominations, for example, the United Church of Christ, the United Methodist Church, the Church of the Brethren, and the United Presbyterian Church, do now ordain women as ministers, the number of women ministers is small and their acceptance in local congregations is questionable. The ministerial search committee of a Midwest Unitarian congregation needing a minister decided to survey its membership in 1973 to determine some of the wishes of the members about the kind of person they would like to have as a pastor and the various services they expected the pastor to render. The committee asked the following questions at separate places on the questionnaire: (1) Do you believe women should be ordained as ministers? and (2) Would you accept a woman minister in our congregation? An overwhelming majority answered "yes" to the first question. Only five percent replied affirmatively to the second question.

Even within the laity it is more common to find men officiating and speaking in worship convocations than women. In several congregations of various denominations women are providing leadership as liturgists or lay readers, but they are not usually sought to present the sermon. One is reminded of Samuel Johnson's observation. He compared a preaching woman to a dog walking on its hind legs: in either case, he said, we ask not how well it is done, but marvel that it can be done at all. A Lutheran female college student reported that in her congregation it is acceptable for female youth of the church to give sermons, but not adult women.

The reasons women either are not encouraged to preach or do not accept that responsibility when asked are complex. In some cases the women may not believe themselves capable of such a task, especially if they are part of a high-church tradition.[9] Though the experience of women in most Protestant churches confirms either deliberate or subtle discrimination against female leadership, women are more often found in leadership capacities in black congregations or in low-church traditions. In black congregations, I am told, there are very few male members who are present or willing to assume leadership responsibilities. A low-church tradition emphasizes emotion, compassion, and service, whereas intellectual, theological discussions are valued highly by a high church. Stereotypically, women are presumed more capable in handling the emotional side of life, thus their leadership might seem more acceptable and natural within low churches. Whatever the reasons in fact are, it is to the advantage of all human beings to know women who do minister in the professional as well as the personal sense.

Even fewer women serve the holy sacraments than function as lay worship leaders. An explanation for the prevailing practice of male officiants, given by many women as well as men, is that the presence of a woman in administering the sacraments, as in worship leadership, is blasphemous at worst and distracting at best. In many cases women church members are more distressed than men when a woman does give a sermon or read the Scriptures. They may view such a woman as an attention-seeker, and often they find her words less credible than if the same words had been spoken by a male.

In a congregation with a female pastor several women became disturbed when, during their own hospitalizations, the female pastor visited them. That, they said, is a job for a man. What must women conclude about their beings when they are held to be blasphemous or distracting by a Christian fellowship? How can women be related genuinely to other sisters when they feel the leadership of women in the worship of the church to be inappropriate?

Because of this apparent judgment against the place of women within the spiritual life of the church, we will understand why many tasks within the church are divided along culturally-accepted sexual lines. Women who have been barred from or have chosen not to lead in the spiritual and intellectual part of church ministry are eagerly sought for the service and nurturant tasks of the church. Generally women tend to the housecleaning functions; they nurse the aging and the ill; they arrange flowers for worship and wedding receptions; and they prepare dinners, sometimes not by desire but by design. Women, even non-mothers, are sought for positions involving care or guidance of children before men, even fathers. Men are looked to for ideas and decisions.

The purpose of pointing out the assignment of tasks along sex lines is to show, in fact, what kinds of tasks we culturally give highest value and how cultural valuation operates in the church's life. Though much lip-service is paid to the great importance of the nurturant role of a mother, of the home, and of the church, we find few men fulfilling that role. Some people argue that because of biology a man is less suited to nurture. I think a more accurate appraisal of the situation is that ideas, rather than caring, function as money does in our culture. Ideas are an acceptable means of trade in a society in which power and worth are associated with intellect.

The nurturant tasks, though verbally revered, do not carry an equivalent monetary or prestige value; thus, simply by being female and having sex-linked expectations placed upon her, a woman's prescribed and acceptable contribution (i.e., child care rather than thought) automatically renders her worth less in social value than a man. A man who finds nurturant tasks fulfilling for him usually must seek a way to get paid for his natural ability in order to make his contribution respectably "masculine." With such sex-linked division of responsibilities everyone loses.

Dividing tasks along sex lines forces us to view women and men as more different than alike, to deny wholeness (the presence of nurturing gentleness *and* alert intellects) to every individual, and to ostracize those people who do not conform to the general sex stereotypes.

The educational activities of the church probably have as much influence as any program either to perpetuate or to cease the kind of sex stereotyping described above, especially for children. Some denominations have examined their church school materials to discover the extent to which the material unfairly reinforces sexual stereotypes. I cite a few of these just briefly.

Miriam Crist and Tilda Norberg have made a study of the United Methodist nursery curriculum. They examined each story, song, or picture for

> evidence of attitudinal bias in the following areas:
> 1. Sex-typing of play activities, behavior and feelings of boys and girls
> 2. the role of mother and father
> 3. evidence of girls helping mothers and boys helping fathers
> 4. occupational sex-typing of men and women.[10]

From the study, the women concluded that

men and boys were generally shown as active, brave, useful, shaping their environment, and happy in their world. Women and girls were portrayed as passive, powerless, waiting, needing help, watching the action, and often unhappy.[11]

The roles fulfilled by mothers and fathers was another area of the children's material examined by Crist and Norberg. Again they found traditional stereotypes supported.

With only one exception, mothers were portrayed in their traditional role of homemaker, child-rearer, and volunteer worker. The exception was a single instance of a working mother—referred to indirectly in a story about mother and father taking a child to a day-care center. In only two instances were there baby-sitters in the home, and in one of those situations it was clearly stated that mother was away only when attending a meeting. This, in spite of the fact that 29 million women in America work, many as the sole family breadwinner.[12]

Lou Ann Talcott designed a similar preliminary study of the Church of the Brethren church school Encounter Series. She reports, among other conclusions, that throughout the preschool materials God is referred to as a male. The presence of men working with children in a nursery class is treated as exceptional. The stories included to be read to children during the class experience support traditional male and female role stereotypes as the following titles reveal: "John's Mother Cares for Him" and "Jimmy's Daddy Works for Him."[13]

Talcott's study includes examination of the teachers' guides as well as the children's materials. From her perusal of the guides she reports that

. . . the director of children's work is male. His job is, among other things, advice-giving to women teachers who feel "helpless and inadequate" (p. 9). Further along a woman teacher admits having never been to the church library. Edna, later, can't stay and evaluate the lesson because her family is waiting and "They'll be starved" (p. 17). At another point one teacher is worrying about a substitute she got for a class the next Sunday. She comments about her husband's reaction: "You know how men think we stew over such little things" (p. 83), . . . I maintain that in these few examples women teachers appear passive, powerless, are waiting on others, and are needing help and protection. . . . Even though this is not curriculum as such, teachers read it, it reinforces traditional ideas and values, and the teachers, then, act as role models for the children whom they teach.[14]

In adult church school classes in which I have participated through the years, I have seen the results of such sex stereotyping. Without exception in sexually integrated classes, men have dominated the discussion. Even in a special interest class conducted on the nature of woman and the social ferment among women today, the men carried the discussion. Men talked about what women are by nature; they enumerated the needs and desires of women. Meanwhile, the majority of women were silent. Even if the men's appraisal of the women in that group was correct, does it not seem unusual that the women should have needed spokesmen for what it means to be female?

The final aspect of church life for us to examine here is the preparation for and celebration of marriage. The church's attitude toward marriage, both the couple's relationship and the ceremony, reveal further the continuation of cultural sex-stereotyping sanctioned by the church. If any marriage counseling is done prior to the wedding ceremony, it is usually handled by a male minister, priest, or rabbi. The needs and goals of the woman are often, according to women who have shared about their own experiences with such counseling, not mentioned except as the woman is gently instructed to be a helpmate for her husband. Such advice is good counsel except that the suggestion goes only one way and is given solely to the woman. Where the husband will work, how he will further his education, and how *he* will provide the income are major issues implicit in which is the assumption that the male will perform such duties alone. Concerns about a woman's career or job are secondary. Any counseling regarding the anticipation or advent of children is usually directed primarily to the woman.

The wedding day is a celebrated moment. Both bride and groom are filled with trust, desire, and love as the father of the bride, in traditional ritual, gives his daughter to the man who will become her husband. This practice of fathers giving away daughters is fraught with paternalistic overtones and treats a woman as a kind of possession to be given and received. The wedding, to the extent that it becomes a display of fashion finery and pageantry, is dominated by women. Men, particularly grooms, often report feeling unneeded on this occasion of public covenant making. How can mutual covenant be proclaimed when bride or groom is treated either as an object for possession or as an appendage?

At the conclusion of the ceremony the bride, who at the beginning of the service was referred to as a separate being with her own name, is attached to her husband and introduced as Mrs. John Jackson. In this brief ceremony she has given up her right in some states to own property, to buy a car, to secure credit without her husband's signature, or to have an independent legal status. In the same exchange a man has taken on responsibility for a dependent adult.

Fortunately, experimentation with the wedding ceremony itself is occurring in several Protestant denominations. In some instances now both parents of the bride and the groom make a statement of their consent and support of the relationship. Similarly, a few insightful clergy people are upholding in the words of the wedding ceremony the integrity and autonomy of two separate individuals making a covenant. One elderly man of wisdom spoke to a couple throughout their ceremony with their separate names, advising them not to lose their separateness, and then introduced them at the conclusion as John Jackson and Mary Jones Jackson, a new union of two people.

The church has used one verse in Ephesians 5 out of context against women in the marriage relationship for years. Taken out of context it fits more nearly secular attitudes, buttressed by reference to such Scriptures, about assumed sexual inequality in marriage. It is such fragmented advice which undergirds Western marriage custom and is, perhaps erroneously, associated with the Apostle Paul. In the case of Ephesians there is serious question about Paul's authorship. Many New Testament scholars think Ephesians was written by a disciple of Paul.[15]

"Wives, be subject to your husbands, as to the Lord" (Ephesians 5:22). Period. That is where the institutional church and Western culture usually stop reading. But the rest of the text about the human marriage relationship is given in Ephesians 5:25: "Husbands, love your wives in the same way that Christ loved the church and gave his life for it." In Ephesians 5:28 we find: "Men ought to love their wives just as they love their own bodies. A man who loves his wife loves himself." The kind of relationship the author is describing here is what Jesus was talking about in Matthew 20:27-28 (KJV) when he said, "And whosoever will be chief among you, let him be your servant: Even as the Son of man came not to be ministered unto, but to minister. . . . "

Anna Mow in *The Secret of Married Love* says to men approaching marriage, "Brace yourself, young man, this really means: a husband is the head of his wife when he is her servant."[16] The New Testament teaching to be "subject to one another is a *chosen* attitude; it is *servanthood* and not *servitude.*"[17] Being subject to one another is Jesus' example for all human relationships, not simply marriage. "You never need be afraid of losing authority . . . in this servanthood of love, for it has nothing to do with cringing, spineless servitude. It is the secret of strength"[18] through which the self and other selves are affirmed. It is the paradoxical power and strength of servanthood that Western culture and much of Christianity does not comprehend. Instead, the church continues to confuse giving in and losing oneself *in* another, rather than *for* another, with giving and serving from mature selfhood. Marriages that are built on the self-denial of one or both individuals ultimately become enslaving for both because neither can experience the liberating power of loving and of being loved.

The irony in the Western view of marriage is that traditional ideas about the submission of women to their husbands are defended by the church as biblically based. However, the biblical marriage covenant, described in parts of the Old Testament and in closer readings of the New Testament, revolutionizes marriage as we have commonly known it in its non-biblical form throughout Christian history. The marriage relationship, often symbolized by Christ's marriage with the church or God's covenant with Israel, can never be one of possession. Instead it must free the participants to be and to become genuinely whole selves, if commitment, even to the point of death, is taken seriously.

Marriage as symbolized by Christ and the church has nothing to do with sex-stereotypes and rigid role expectations traditionally adopted by most couples during marriage. Within Western culture marriage has in practice often been a legal means of possessing one another in a relationship that is like a heavy yoke on each; such a burden is not covenant as expressed in Jesus' life. The liberation one should experience through the marriage covenant, whether made between one man and one woman or between and among many individuals, enables one to reach to the mate in total openness and outward to others with a spirit of servanthood and covenant. When carried far enough this suggests the "marriage" of all human beings.

What might we conclude about the church as a liberator or an oppressor of women from the preceding commentary drawn from the experiences of Christian women? That women might feel confusion in their relationship to the church seems undeniable. Through the language of the Scriptures, the liturgies, the hymns and prayers of the church, women learn as children that it is a man's kingdom on earth and apparently in heaven. They, whose lives biologically and emotionally (both by social prescription and by choice) are related closely with mystery in the life process, who are described as intuitive and appreciative of matters spiritual, are not encouraged to minister in a professional sense. They are guided, in and outside the church, to do the all-important work of nurturing and serving for which they are then ignored or even belittled.

Because of rigid separation of thinking and serving, women's minds are isolated and men's capacities for caring underdeveloped. In the educational materials that predominantly women use to teach the young, the women see their sex described as helpless, passive, and unhappy. And they unconsciously shape the little girls in their classes to fit that mold. From puzzling and oft misrepresented scriptural injunctions (Paul's advice about asceticism) they conclude that marriage to a man is their most direct route to social acceptability and Christian salvation. Are these conditions liberating for women? If not so for women, can men find in them anything but oppression that is born of separation, female from male, and domination, male over female?

What, one is surely led to ask, are the roots of these practices that divide man from woman, pit woman against woman, and most importantly deny full personhood to women as well as men? Is this the garden God intends for us to inhabit?

Into My Own *(The inner life, when we dare to touch that place, gives us what Robert Frost said poetry gave to him—"a momentary stay against the confusion of the world." Into My Own is an invitation to that place.)*

Do you remember hearing about the church-related experiences of your mother or grandmother? What were/are her attitudes toward the church? What about your father or grandfather?

Study some of your favorite hymns. What makes them special to you?

If you try to alter some of the male pronouns (that refer to all human beings) in hymns, what do you experience?

You might want to write a letter (as if to your daughter, son, or friend) sharing personally the ways in which God is active in your life and the call you think God makes toward us.

Chapter 2.

WORSHIPING THE
FALLEN CREATION

"I heard the sound of thee in the garden, and I was afraid, because I was naked; and I hid myself" (Genesis 3:10).

In the 1960s Eric Berne's *Games People Play* became a popular book and offered a new technique for talking about our interpersonal transactions. The analysis of games in American life has encouraged some self-understanding and has helped us develop a sense of humor about the character of our human exchanges. What we have not comprehended as well is the relationship between game-playing and oppression. What do our games with one another tell us about ourselves and the way we view our world?

For women within the Christian church the reality of oppression—described as an experience of being ignored, of feeling less worthy than men, of passively fulfilling non-thinking roles, of seeking to know a God as a distant abstraction or as carved out in male images—is both the result and the perpetuating cause of a large-scale social game I have come to call "Squash." Few of us escape some form of this game which we play in varied ways to hide our nakedness (our real selves) from our own and one another's gazes. Although "Squash" is most easily witnessed on the interpersonal level, as we additionally examine its institutionalized forms we begin to understand a world view that has created the separation and oppression that plague our lives within the church and the society.

"Squash" operates in two areas simultaneously: the external and the internal. On the external level it is a game of competition. It can be played with friendly vigor, in which case friends vie with one another to outshine each other; some would call this the healthy spirit of competition. In my small town it is difficult to find women who are very different from one another, though much energy is expended by women seeking to define themselves more persuasively than their friends. For example, Ms. A. decides to get a part-time job; soon Mses. B, C, and D also are looking for part-time work. Or Ms. X may decide to take some classes at a nearby educational institution, sometimes for credit, sometimes for personal enrichment. Before long the idea seems good to Mses. Y and Z.

In personal decoration this practice of competition or "Squash" has been evident for centuries and exploited profitably by designers and merchandisers. Ms. J. has her hair coiffed in the latest style at the most popular boutique; soon Mses. K, L, and M cannot appear at the company dinner without being similarly combed and clothed. To the extent that each of these women's actions are independent and personally life-enriching, one could argue for their important, healthy value. If, on the other hand, they are attempts to imitate or to elevate oneself by subtly squashing another person, they do harm to one's own being and one's capacity for relationship.

"Squash" may also be played with intense malice, in which case persons are defamed by vituperative attacks on fellow human beings. Cartoons and jokes abound to stereotype women over coffee cups drinking uncertain toasts to their neighbor's cluttered house, her unruly children, or her unusual ideas. It is tragically too easy for us to think of examples when we ourselves or our friends may have been misrepresented or belittled by others seeking power, self-justification, or recognition.

On the inner level, that area of ourselves that we know least well and sometimes listen to not at all, "Squash" is a game of pleading. "Squash" is played by the psychologically and intellectually powerless, those who have given up their minds and their spirits to the conforming majority. It is my guess that a significant percentage of women and men have played variations of this game at some time in their lives; therefore, to generalize about any psychological sensations one receives when playing "Squash" is impossible. But I suspect one derives a temporary feeling of power or satisfaction from successfully gaining advantage, even if only in one's own mind and for a fleeting moment, over another, perhaps equally powerless, human being. A sense of entrapment and futility arises, though, when the transitory feeling of achievement received at another's expense leaves and one again needs to repeat the game.

It is easy for us to acknowledge the presence of "Squash" in our casual relationships, but we squirm to consider how we play "Squash" in our intimate encounters. In the most intimate human relationship, one chosen by a woman and a man, "Squash" is played, though sometimes less deliberately than in other human relationships, whenever either person exploits the other by responding to her or him as a fixed being. Whenever one responds to the other as only body or principally mind, a variety of "Squash" is at work.

Whenever either person is taken for granted and no longer actively cherished, whenever growth experiences are assumed to be essential for only one of the persons in the relationship, whenever either one's personhood is reduced to a role or to meeting external expectations, whenever both persons are gradually turned inward, dependent on themselves alone, cut off from a larger community that enriches their individual beings and enlarges their loving, "Squash" is operating. These conditions prevail in a vast number of relationships between women and men today.

"Squash" is able to take hold of our personal and inter-personal lives in large part because it is strongly supported by institutions in the culture. American public education is one of the most influential social institutions; the skills and factual knowledge we teach the young seem often of second-ary importance to a general attitude about and the stance toward life that we instill.

What are the values that we hold before students more by our own actions than by our philosophies? We encourage learning to occur through a system of competition that carries with it sophisticated means of gratification and the withdrawal of gratification. The goal of competitive educa-tion is to arrive earliest at the highest level of social accep-tability. In order to achieve such a goal the individual is re-quired to reject or to repress some part of her or his being that is different from an accepted social model.

The mass nature of public education makes social con-formism a higher value than individuality. For a child, ex-ploring the unknown often becomes a Squash-like encounter of acquiring power over information and winning com-petitively over one's peers. The pressure on the young and powerless is to secure a place for their beings in an often an-tagonistic environment.

Perhaps the most obvious form of institutionalized "Squash" occurs in an economy dependent on consumerism and motivated by profit-making. With the aid of the institu-tion of advertising we learn passively what we are supposed to need, want, and deserve, in order to compete personally with other human beings. We have come to accept businesses whose primary interest is to insure profit and only secondarily to serve genuine human need.

In domestic politics and foreign policy game-playing is commonplace. To squash a political opponent by acceptable and questionable means, by legal and illegal campaign con-tributions, is to be rewarded with an office of social honor. Foreign policy may be a large-scale power game. The desire and need to play "Squash" by any nation come from beliefs in self-righteousness and "Manifest Destiny."

In short, "Squash" arises from, and further creates, feelings of disunity with others and mistrust of oneself. The feelings of disunity and mistrust develop early in our lives and are exacerbated by the disintegration of families and communities that, at an earlier time, had some cohesive influence on individual lives and social relations. The disunity and mistrust that make "Squash" nearly an inevitable response to life have been fostered also by the Christian church and stem from two sources at least: (1) a divided worldview rooted in apocalyptic Judaism and Neoplatonism,[1] and (2) general ignorance of the meaning and function of myth in biblical cultures and in reshaping the present. The first of these two sources of dislocation we will take up in the remainder of this chapter. We will look at the second source as a route leading away from the worship of the fallen creation and toward experiences of wholeness in creation in chapter 3.

Greek philosophic dualism has given us all the basic dualities —

> the alienation of the mind from the body; the alienation of the subjective self from the objective world; the subjective retreat of the individual, alienated from the social community; the domination or rejection of nature by spirit[2]

that undergird our notions about ourselves and the world. In any dualism wholeness is split in two, and tension between often warring parts results in conditions of domination and submission, acceptance and rejection between the parts of the divided object or person.

The mind-body division has alienated individuals from themselves, woman from man, and human beings from the divine. It is this dualism, acted out concretely as the irreconcilable separation of woman and man, that is the prototype of the other dualities mentioned above. How do we experience this duality within our individual beings? Alan Watts described the effects of division in one being.

> The body is so alien to the mind that even when it is at its best it is not so much loved as exploited, and for the remainder of the time we do what we may to put it in a state of comfort where it may

be forgotten, where its limitations will not encumber the play of emotion and thought.[3]

The mind-body duality operates in the perennial struggle of woman and man because of the associations of each sex with either pole of this division: male with mind, female with body. Such association in the Christian church was most strongly influenced by Gnosticism, a movement of the Hellenistic age. With the Gnostics came a heightened contempt for the life of the flesh and a desire to seek salvation from the material (fleshly) world through "divine illumination and superior knowledge (gnosis) or wisdom."[4] The Divine was above the material world and to be protected from contamination of human contact.

> So far as sex is concerned, the Gnostics were divided into two camps: extreme asceticism and extreme libertinism. The motivation to the former seems obvious enough. . . . If the flesh was evil, the less one had to do with it the better. It was part of the realm of the devil, and those who fell prey to its tempting wills suffered death of the soul as well as death of the body. This school of Gnostics preached virginity and celibacy, and looked upon marriage as an inferior estate. All sex suffered from a dual liability. It aroused material lusts and it resulted in imprisoning further souls in bodies through procreation. This was a viewpoint not confined to the Gnostics, and the New Testament reflects both Christian attraction and Christian hostility to such an attitude.[5]

The early Christian church strongly rejected Gnostic libertinism and attempted to oppose dualism and extreme asceticism. Although the Christian community had its roots in Jewish practice and faith, which affirmed the material world as God's creation, it also had a vision of an imminent, coming kingdom. Thus, we find conflicting views about human sexuality expressed in the New Testament.

> Paul clearly had to deal in Corinth with those who regarded all sexuality as wicked and sinful, as well as with those who looked upon it as morally indifferent. He refused to sanction either extreme. Sex, like everything else in life, was to be consecrated to the service of God. It could be given up by those who sought to please the Lord, devoting the whole of their energies to that enterprise. But it could also be used in the household of faith without sin if it was carried on in love and fidelity.[6]

That Paul, because he believed in the imminence of the kingdom, preferred that Christians choose celibacy seems clear in 1 Corinthians 7:1-7 and 38. The implication still remains in Cole's above analysis that one pleases the Lord better by devoting her or his total energies to Christian service than by marrying or following the needs of the flesh. Such emphasis on preferring the spirit over the body has encouraged Christians, since the time of Paul, to feel divided in their beings. Though indeed there is an attempt by the early church to avoid total rejection of sexuality, we also find spirituality exalted above the flesh. And so the dualism between mind and body has remained potent for two thousand years.

From the Genesis 3 story of the fall, reflected in 1 Timothy 2:11-15, we find reinforced a view of woman as transgressor, as the channel for evil who can be redeemed only through her ties to the earth (the bearing of children) and in submission to her husband. Such thought has given continued impetus to the notion that woman belongs to the body side of the mind-body duality and man to the mind part. It is woman as seductress, as the so-called transgressor Eve, from whom man needs to free himself through dominance.

What has this primary dualism meant for women throughout history? Women are caught in a double bind; those who have grown up with Gnostic influence may try to repress their sexuality. At the same time, we live in a culture that seeks to exploit the sexuality of its female members, so that women also feel compelled to treat their physical bodies as objects for adornment. In both situations, sexuality is undervalued and not integrated into whole persons.

Those women who try to repress their physical sexuality may do so by seeking a life of spirituality. A symptom of repressed sexuality is the guilt that occurs whenever one experiences evidences of femaleness, such as menstruation or physical arousal in the presence of a man. Women who have learned to know themselves primarily as sex objects follow the dictates of the culture and paint, perfume, and generally prepare themselves for the pleasure of men. Often these women reject their natural beauty for aids that hide the real and perfect the artificial. The majority of women find themselves trapped between repressing sexuality and giving heightened attention to their sexual attractiveness. In both cases they have been cut off from themselves as wholesome bodies that also incorporate minds into their beings.

The irony of a woman's situation throughout a history influenced by classical dualism is that the fleshly part of life contains the womb of life through which human birth occurs and recurs. Although in this way women are closely linked to creation and mystery, the instruction of the Christian church and of Western society has been that fleshliness is evil. In carrying dualistic reasoning in this area to its logical conclusion, both women and men have grown to assume that earth-linked, flesh-related processes are embarrassing and somewhat sinister.

Perhaps because the fleshly intimacy necessary for pleasure and for procreation has been viewed as a less worthy endeavor for human beings than seeking to perfect the spirit, we have in the New Testament a witness given to pregnancies created by the Holy Spirit. With a wholistic world view, would it not seem possible that the Spirit of God would be incarnate in the physical as well as spiritual union of a female and a male? In Hebrew societies

> sex was not to [the Hebrews] a mere amorous dalliance, a game to be played part way and then abandoned. They took their sex seriously as an activity involving pleasure and peril, recreation and responsibility.[7]

Thus, when Sarah and Abraham were without a child, the interpreted intervention by God in Sarah's pregnancy was a sign of blessing for the couple. Sex and procreation were sacred parts of the wholeness of life.

The tragedy for women, from which there has been little escape within the Christian church, is that their beings have been limited to body, and bodiliness has been looked on with contempt. Despite the goodness that concrete women feel in being human, sexual, procreative beings, their feelings of goodness have been devalued. Furthermore, many women have never been acknowledged as whole beings that include mind and spirit as well as body. Thus, women themselves have become mistrustful of their own beings and have fulfilled external prescriptions set for them by not thinking and not seeking, but by passively absorbing, the definition given them as sometimes helper, sometimes seductress, but always a little less worthy than the male.

For men, the mind/body dualism has meant dominance over the world and particularly over the rejected side of human unity: the female. The image of God in the West is similar to the Greek male warrior. Men have identified with the might and majesty of God and have fought against all kinds of evils believed to be antagonistic to the power of God. The feminine aspects included in some of the images of various tribal gods of the Mediterrean world are absent from the traditional concept we have of Yahweh. Even the metaphors that contain female allusions when speaking about God are rarely referred to in the worship or education of the Christian church.

The church's ignorance of the female qualities attributed to Yahweh in the Old Testament bears testimony to our alienation from a wholistic God. The presence of female imagery in the Scriptures forces us to accept that some people possessed non-patriarchal vision centuries ago. In Numbers 11:12 Moses cries out angrily against God:

> Did I conceive all this people? Did I bring them forth, that thou shouldst say to me, "Carry them in your bosom, as a nurse carries the sucking child, to the land which thou didst swear to give their fathers?" (Numbers 11:12).

The implication of Yahweh as mother is clear. In Isaiah 42:14b Yahweh describes birth pangs, "now I will cry out like a woman in travail, I will gasp and pant." Again in Isaiah 49:15 God compares her compassion for Zion to a mother:

> Can a woman forget her sucking child,
>   that she should have no compassion on the son of her womb?

> Even these may forget,
>   yet I will not forget you.[8]

The strongest anti-female evidence I have heard came from living men who have repeatedly disclosed their discomfort about relating to the historic Jesus. His so-called "feminine" qualities of gentleness, compassion, and forgiveness rather than aggression and domination make him an unlikely model for Western men.

Living with a divided world view requires one person in a couple relationship to be subordinate to the other. The effect of the mind/body division on human sexual relationships has been to make union in a wholistic sense impossible. The Genesis 2:4b-25 Yahwistic narrative of creation has generally been interpreted by the Christian church as divine justification for patriarchy as a social order. Man is created first, and when his loneliness is not mitigated by the creation of various forms of animal life, God creates a "helper" fit for him. Reading with eyes dimmed by patriarchy, we assume that woman is second, therefore lesser in creation, and that she is designed to serve by being a "helper fit for man." In man's acknowledgement of woman

> This is at last bone of my bones
>   and flesh of my flesh;
> she shall be called Woman,
>   because she was taken out of Man (Genesis 2:23).

there is presumed control over the woman by the man as he names her.

The patriarchal social order and the dualistic rejection of sexuality are further supported in church doctrine taken from the story of the fall, for which woman is blamed and from which there is eternal ejection from paradise, and the presence of shame between woman and man. Paul's comment in 1 Corinthians 11:3, "But I want you to understand that the head of every man is Christ, the head of a woman is her husband, and the head of Christ is God," reflects both the church's and the society's identification with male dominance as a divinely ordained hierarchy.

Because the mind/body division is of greatest

significance for the subject of female oppression in the Christian church we have given more intensive attention to it than we will to the alienation of the subjective self from the objective world, the alienation of the subjective individual from the social community, and the domination or rejection of nature. However, we cannot ignore these three dualities since they are complexly tied with the mind/body duality and give further evidence of a fallen creation to which we have bowed.

One of the characteristic marks of nineteenth and twentieth century life is the prevailing belief in objectivity. By objectivity we mean the ability to hold objects, situations, and persons at a distance so as to evaluate them isolated and of themselves alone, with as little involvement of subjective influences as possible. In a subjective/objective tension, what one feels or thinks inwardly is always subject to what one perceives objectively in the world outside, the outer dimension of life, so to speak. And the subjective self is usually altered to mesh with the objective world rather than to shape it.

We can check the degree to which we are rejecting the subjective self by how much we listen to our inner beings, by how much attention we give to our personal fantasies and to the social myths through which we express our deepest longings, and by how torn we feel when a conflict arises between the subjective self and the expectations of the external world. The split between our inner selves and the outer world tends to remove us from the objective world by placing us in mistrustful tension with it. That which we mistrust we either avoid or seek to dominate. Either response makes us unlikely to see ourselves as a part of all that is in the world.

One of the factors contributing to the rejection of our subjective selves is that we are largely separated from meaningful social communities. In societies that were based on strong extended families, one achieved his or her identity through the clan relationships. There was a common history shared by the clan members, a set of agreed-upon norms, and rites that repeatedly unified the community.[9] The relationships within the clan offered support for the individual and through such support made her or his individuality, the expression of her or his subjective self, possible.

In contrast to the extended families or the covenant communities of the Old Testament (see, for example, Exodus 19—24), we live within separated nuclear family units that are part of a fragmented society. There are few corporate norms that we, even within a particular congregation of any denomination, might agree upon. And our histories seem so disparate that they usually go unshared. Furthermore, having been reared on social individualism we are not sure that corporate norms or covenant communities are in our own personalized interests. Thus we float, unattached to others who care for us and alienated from the essence of life which is self and community actualization through relationship. That is to say, life for individuals apart from community is impossible.

In the long run, aloneness becomes alienation; and then disintegration, psychological or physical, of individual life takes place. The purpose in discussing the alienation of the self from the social community is to demonstrate from a different point of view the movement necessary in life for reunion to replace separation.

Our separation from primary community relationships has allowed us to pursue our private wishes with few restraints. The prevailing belief in the supreme rights of the human individual has created the conditions in which the rape of the natural world could occur. Human beings, believing themselves to be separate from and higher in the hierarchy of creation than trees, foxes, flowers, and bushes, have interpreted the words in Genesis

> . . . and let them have dominion over the fish of the sea, and over the birds of the air, and over the cattle, and over all the earth, and over every creeping thing that creeps upon the earth (Genesis 1:26)

to mean that humanity should have control or power over nature. We view nature as phenomena outside human experience, a combination of objects to be used by human beings.

The rape of nature is perhaps understandable when we see the parallels that exist between the mind/body dualism and the dualism of humanity against nature. The creative and recreative cycles of the natural world, akin to the procreative capacities of the female, are mindless and therefore less than man. Cut off from the intimacy and unity of female and male, divided even within the self, separated from community identity, human beings are also alienated from nature. Relationship of any kind seems impossible in the fallen creation. The environmental problem central in our concern now is, in the final analysis, a relational worldview problem. If people had understood themselves as a part of the air and the water, for example, would they easily have polluted the streams with debris and blackened the air with noxious smoke from profit-puffing industries? If people had felt the needs of others as their own, through community covenants, would there have been inner restraints on the desire to waste and to exploit?

Probably the most alarming result of our personal and corporate alienation is being studied now by neuropsychologists, like James Prescott, who believe there are significant linkages between the rejection of physical contact (at all ages) and the production of aggression and violence in a society. In societies where the young are not cuddled and the sexuality of the adolescents is repressed or denied by rigid moral codes, Prescott suggests that we can expect to find aggressive, violent behavior as a personal and social characteristic.[10]

Perhaps the antagonism, the repressed hostility we experience between the sexes, which we call opposites, is grounded in our unmet basic needs for touch and for open acknowledgement of our sexuality. As our needs for touch and accepted sexuality are fulfilled, we may begin to view the sexes as complementary for the first time, and strangers as sisters or brothers.

Our dualistic world view denies life; it leaves life in the fallen state as we struggle ever more strenuously at "Squash" to stay alive in some fashion. The world that we perceive with limited vision and live in is a fallen world. We worship the fallen world described *but not justified* at the end of the Genesis 3 story of the fall where human beings are separated from God; man and woman know shame between them; the lush vegetation of the garden has turned to thorns and thistles, and man is condemned to toil in the dry fields; woman is required to bear children in pain; and mutuality and union are no longer present in either human relationships or in human-divine relationships.

To the extent that we move God above and beyond human experience, limit our God to human male images, ignore the divine presence in nature and in human life, we are worshiping a fallen creation. When we reject our own sexuality and exploit the beings of the complementary sex by viewing another person as only a half being, when we accept and participate in hierarchies that squash the lives of others, when we refuse relationship in preference for individualism, when we reject our inner beings in order to fit external molds, we are worshiping a fallen creation. The fallen creation that we label as belonging to God and as part of God's plan for life creates in us the restlessness of alienation. We have a vague sense amidst our personal, social, and religious turmoil that indeed the thistles have taken over the land and that the garden, the very core of life, needs recultivation. How do we rename and reclaim the garden?

Into My Own

Make a list of the ways you have played, or have observed, "Squash." Can you remember any of your feelings on those occasions?

What is your understanding of the Genesis story of the fall? Reread Genesis 3. What importance does it have in your life?

Chapter 3.

THE ROLE OF MYTH
IN RENAMING THE GARDEN

I know who I am and may become if I choose. —Don Quixote

The perpetuation of a fallen creation is possible because we have lost contact with myth. Because the word *myth* commonly conjures up images of falsehood, magic, visions, or insanity, we try to hold myth at a distance so as not to be deceived. We seem to be unaware that finally in our attempt to deny the function of myth in our personal and corporate lives, we become more alienated from ourselves and from one another.

An important function of myth has always been to help people imagine the unseen, release their fears of the unknown, and create a sense of security in the face of foreboding change. The story of Hansel and Gretel has helped many children, through its mythic form, to deal with their univerbalized fears about being rejected by an unloving stepmother, about getting lost in their own dark forests, surrounded by eerie noises and spooky shadows and without food. The outcome of that myth is reunion; having made the venture through the maze of lostness and aloneness, Hansel and Gretel bake the witch in her own oven and are reunited with home.

Many of us are unacquainted with the power and necessity of myths. In our twentieth-century preoccupation with scientific verification we have forgotten about the mythic power of Red Riding Hood and the wolf, Jonah and the whale, Rumpelstiltskin, or even Eve and the garden serpent. We fail to understand the role of fantasy in arbitrating against our insecurities. In an age of science, myths seem incredible and childish. We have convinced ourselves that they are falsehoods, exaggerated tales that should be left behind us. One purpose of this chapter is to explore myth as a means of revealing truth, not in the realm of the material world but in a spiritual or psychical sense. A second purpose is to suggest ways in which we lose touch with myth and, consequently, think of myth as falsehood.

Despite its current existence in a fallen creation, the human soul inherently yearns to experience wholeness. Whether in primitive cultures, where the human imagination was consumed with fantasies, or in the present, where imagination is kept in strict check by reason, people have expressed a longing for unity with their own depths and with the universe. From primitive cultures we have fantastic myths of nymphs and gorgons that give voice to the inner experiences of the unknown in the lives of the people.

In contemporary civilization, largely cut off from mythic experience, we find ourselves instead in one of several conditions: we fear the inner unknown and therefore control it by a consciousness whose tool is reason; we attempt to plumb our internal worlds by means of personal analysis; or we seek corporate support for our inward journey through sensitivity and therapy groups of all varieties. If we are individually attentive to an inner life at all, we struggle in vain to get in contact with it through the use of intellect alone, and the pervasive sense of mental disquiet unnerves us.

What is the source of our restlessness? The problem for

modern women and men is not that we have intellectual paralysis but that we live without imagination. Our lives are not merely incomplete because of our unquestioned commitment to reason; they are barren, and we feel desolate and alone in spite of our strenuous attempts to know ourselves and to be in touch with others.

A number of years ago the book, *Don Quixote,* changed my life, rather drastically I suspect. The longer I live with that book and its principal character, the more I am convinced that the uneasiness we experience in the modern world is closely akin to the restlessness that led an obscure author in Spain in the 1600s to create a character who still waits to be understood by contemporary human beings.

Cervantes' *Don Quixote,* released in 1605 in Madrid, portrayed the tension between the eternal realities of a barren, lonely life for a fifty-year-old common man and his inner world, between the mundane and the sacred, between the empirical and the imaginative. Don Quixote's seventeenth-century world was a money-mad world filled with mule drivers and merchants. It was a secular world without dignity; it was a skeptical world lacking in imagination and faith. These conditions of life, observed by Cervantes, seem hauntingly similar to the tensions of the modern world. They remind us of the uneasy feeling we have that our lives are not merely incomplete; they are empty, though filled with things. I believe that the lack of imagination Cervantes describes in his novel is likewise the source of our own anxiety and alienation.

Throughout the novel Don Quixote tries to actualize his inwardness. That is to say, he acts out his dreams, his visions, his ideals in the external world. He uses his imagination, his dreams about what he is and wants to be, to transform reality. Consequently, he is able to undertake his sallies riding on a hack of a horse that he calls, and believes to be, a prancing charger. An ordinary, misshapen basin set on his head becomes a fine helmet befitting a gallant knight. It is Don Quixote's ability and decision to act "as if" things were as he wishes them that gives his life sense and personal order. Through the "as if" process he transforms his sterile life into a varied, exciting adventure.

Don Quixote is obsessed with naming. He meditates often, "What shall I name?" This concern with naming the world to fit what is inside him points up the intimate relationship between language and being human. To be able to name is to be a more developed human being. Naming brings into existence. And the ability to name is, as Don Quixote shows us, vitalized by the imagination. Without the life of the imagination we are doomed to existences that reflect the world rather than create it.

One of the creations of the human imagination, which simultaneously functions to keep the imagination alive and one's life anchored, is myth. Myth, rather than veiling reality, reaches our greatest human needs and touches the core of our beings. Myths arise from the consciousness and unconsciousness of people; they cannot exist apart from a myth-maker, one who creates and/or recognizes its power in her own life. Myths are the means through which human beings have tried to deal with their longings. Elizabeth Janeway says that myth arises out of " . . . the inability to control one's life . . . it clings to remembered happiness and dreams of its renewal in a new order of things."[1]

Myth mediates the tension between the external and the internal. When you want to cope with the unknown, whether that unknown is outside yourself or within, you may create or adopt a myth which aids in making sense out of the unintelligible. The created myth can be shared with others; as it is shared, it is altered and takes on the insights, expansions, and interpretations of its contributors. Jerome Bruner describes myth as both "at once an external reality and the resonance of the internal vicissitudes of man[2]."[3]

Perhaps most importantly, myth is "a mode of perception that discovers and reveals the bond between man and what he considers sacred."[4] This definition of myth moves us far away from myth as falsehood. The Old Testament writers seem to have accepted their need to give mythic shape to their inner struggles and longings. Their stories became a source of community security and a foundation for action or faithfulness in the face of uncertainty. We trust ourselves and myth less. Within each of us are the longings described by Janeway, aspirations and fears that result in part from repressed ugliness, and perceptions or insights that might help us transcend ourselves.

Because we have not been taught to look within ourselves for a source of truth or of the sacred, we know little about our private inner beings or the collective human consciousness. However, as we pay attention to and trust our inner experiences we are able to respond affirmatively or negatively to ancient myths, to evaluate the helpfulness of legends that have traditionally explained the nature of the world or particular social and religious practices, and to create our own stories about ourselves and the world that honestly reflect our experiences. Without the capacities, latent within ourselves, to respond to and to create myths, we will possibly live only external, half-lives.

Joseph Campbell describes four functions of myth. The first function he defines as " . . . the mystical or metaphysical function of linking regular waking consciousness with the vast mystery of the universe." Who has not in waking moments pondered the meaning of the universe and felt swallowed up in the mystery of its creation? At those moments you may find meaning by reference to traditional myths about the beginning of life such as are recorded in Genesis 1:1: "In the beginning God created the heavens and the earth," or are found in the words of Hesiod, the first Greek who tried to explain how things began:

> Earth, the beautiful, rose up,
> Broad-bosomed, she that is the steadfast base
> Of all things. And fair Earth first bore
> The starry Heaven, equal to herself,
> To cover her on all sides and to be
> A home forever for the blessed gods.[5]

You may, on the other hand, in your own way, with your private hopes and fears bring into being an individual myth that serves to relate you to the vast mystery.

Campbell continues by suggesting that "the cosmological function [of myth] is to present some intelligible image of nature." Again the creation narratives in Genesis have functioned historically in just this way for Judeo-Christian people—to give some comprehensible view of how the natural world was formed. Certain myths of science, for example ones about the shape of the world or the position of the earth in relation to other solar objects, provided in the past some ordering explanation of the natural world.

"The sociological function [of myth] validates and enforces specific social and moral order." Many cultures historically have had initiation rites by which the personal and social progression from childhood to adulthood was carried forward in an orderly fashion. Many of the ideas found in the Declaration of Independence and in the American Constitution have come from the inner longings and dreams about human dignity and independence, and these shared myths, transferred to documents, have held American society together for two centuries.

Finally, "the psychological function [of myth] provides a pathway to conduct individuals through life."[6] Myth ultimately enables you to believe in the value of experience, your inner uniqueness, from which you do not flee but move toward, with the anticipation of discovering the sacredness of your life. Myth permits one to live creatively with the tension between the external and internal realities and gives Quixote-like courage for one to live "as if." Only as we have a sense of "as if" can we transform ourselves. By living "as if,"

> . . . the opaque weight of the world—both of life on earth and of death, heaven, and hell—is dissolved, and the spirit freed, not *from* anything, for there was nothing from which to be freed except a myth too solidly believed, but *for* something, something fresh and new, a spontaneous act.[7]

Our ability to imagine, to conduct ourselves imaginatively toward personhood makes self-transformation possible. Once in touch with our inner longings, our dreams (the unconscious as well as conscious fantasies), our visions, we act "as if" those can be shared outside ourselves. Religious faith is the highest kind of "as if" experience. What Christ's earliest disciples and converts knew in common was that their faith had made them whole, well, or new beings. Without that faith to assume that Christ would touch them, they would perhaps have floundered forever. Similarly, it is our ability to have that kind of faith in our own redeemed goodness and loveliness that makes it possible for us courageously to envision and to create a different, more humanized external reality.

When I have asked churchwomen about the relevance of myth in their lives, the majority overwhelmingly refer to myth as enslaving, an illusion that cloaks the truth. So far I have discussed myth as serving a positive need in our lives, in fact, as a route to Truth. What has occurred to change myth from being a guide to Truth to being a cloak over Truth?

Perhaps the most ambiguous influence on modern culture has been the scientific method. It has permitted contemporary human beings to understand the universe in ways undreamed by earlier beings, yet it has also rendered the mythic capacity obsolete. During the short span of a fertile century the area of the unknown has been vastly decreased. The marvelous accomplishments of science and technology have urged us to see the world and to judge our experiences in it as phenomena which can be empirically verified or which, if they cannot, must therefore be disregarded or discarded. As scientists and archaeologists offered new theories about the origins of the earth, people found it less easy and often naive to accept the biblical accounts of creation. For many people the biblical story lost credibility not because it had no truth but because the readers expected scientific evidence where myth existed. Whatever did not withstand the tests of empiricism tended to be dumped into falsehood.

We subjected myths to various kinds of truth or reality checks, and we found them wanting. Of course, Jack didn't climb a real beanstalk, nor was Little Red Riding Hood's grandmother eaten by a wolf, only to come unscathed from its stomach. We now suspect that the world was not created in six days nor was Eve literally shaped from a rib in a man's (Adam's) side. And Jonah probably could not have survived inside the whale. When the myths didn't fit the tests we did one of two things: either we judged the myth false and useless, or we tried to make the myths literal reports of historic events. In either response we lost touch with the truth-serving power of myth.

Myths are not historic reports of actual events; they are not rigid prescriptive guides for decision-making and conduct. They are interior maps, as it were. Carl Jung, in his *Answer to Job,* distinguishes physical truth from psychic truth, concluding that both are equally important but each reveals a different kind of truth. Myths are instruments that lead us to psychic, or spiritual, truth. They show us the inner experiences or responses human beings make to their external circumstances, which, of course, may be quite verifiable.

If we believe that there are some common threads among humanity, cross culturally as well as across historic eras, we can learn something about our kind in earlier times from ancient myths. The capacity that makes it possible for one to learn from ancient myths is essential for appreciating the inner lives of our contemporaries, especially those with different cultural, religious, or value systems. The imaginative capacity to venture into the unknown areas of the self, others, or the experiences of the Spirit, is essential for myth to survive and function as a means of relating us to the world. An illustration of this capacity at work on an ancient myth will serve well.

Phyllis Trible, a theologian at Andover-Newton Seminary, has written an important reinterpretation of the creation myths of the Old Testament. Her study not only depatriarchalizes the stories, an important contribution in itself, but also helps contemporary persons to perceive anew the nature and power of myth. By highlighting her scholarship we find some directions for reevaluating the importance of myth and for renaming the garden in which we live.

Though Hebrew writings do support patriarchy as the dominant social order, there are many variations within the patriarchal form that show the influence and importance of the female in Hebrew life. Therefore, we should not reject all Old Testament literature because of its patriarchal overtones, and we can look to it decisively for its revelation about myth and human experience. The study of Hebrew culture is helpful in considering the importance of myth because the Hebrews were people tied to the material world.

In contrast to the Gnostics, for example, the Hebrews did not reject their earthliness; instead their stories rose out of their earthy experiences and expressed their longings for a better life. Abstractions, whether applied to Yahweh or given as the basis of ethical living, are uncommon in Hebrew writing. Thus, if one characteristic of living myth is its tie to real people, we can turn to the biblical myths with confidence.

With a lack of mythic insight many feminists are outraged by the Yahwist story of creation and the fall in Genesis 2 and 3. Both the nineteenth-century suffragette Elizabeth Cady Stanton and Sheila D. Collins in 1972 acknowledge that Genesis 1:26-28 depicts woman and man as equal in creation, and they attack Genesis 2 for its debasement of woman. Reared in a patriarchal culture on patriarchal history and religion, their and our outrage is understandable. But is there not evidence that many of us have been too easily misled by the patriarchs, and that by simply bemoaning patriarchal interpretations of the Genesis 2 and 3 stories we permit patriarchy to hold sway on our contemporary consciousness?

Trible begins her exegesis of Genesis 2 and 3 not with the standard eyes of the patriarchy but instead with eyes bent to see in what ways the Genesis 2 and 3 stories may break with patriarchy. She feels justified in beginning from such a standpoint because of themes throughout the Old Testament which appear to be disavowals of sexism. One of those themes is Israel's theological understanding of Yahweh.[8]

Here is a deity set apart from the fertility gods of the ancient Near

> East; a deity whose worship cannot tolerate a cult of sexuality; a deity described as one, complete, whole, and thus above sexuality. . . . As Creator and Lord, Yahweh embraces and transcends both sexes.[9]

Another theme that appears to reject sexism is the prevalent use of female, as well as male, imagery to talk about Yahweh. In the preceding chapter we listed several passages that employ female imagery.

Still another theme that undermines the sexism we so easily expect to find in the Bible is the liberation motif primary in the Exodus.

> . . . the story does teach that the God of Israel abhors slavery; that Yahweh acts through human agents to liberate. . . ; that liberation is a refusal of the oppressed to participate in an unjust society and thus it involves a withdrawal; and that liberation begins in the home of the oppressor. More especially, women nurture the revolution. The Hebrew midwives disobey Pharaoh. His own daughter thwarts him, and her maidens assist. This Egyptian princess schemes with female slaves, mother and daughter, to adopt a Hebrew child whom she names Moses. As the first to defy the oppressor, women *alone* take the initiative which leads to deliverance. (See Exodus 1:15—2:10.)[10]

Because of these themes that reject sexism, Trible commences to reread (not to rewrite) Genesis 2 and 3 and asserts that the Genesis 2 narrative indeed does break with patriarchy. She undertakes the reinterpretation of Genesis 2 and 3 by juxtaposing it with the poetry of the Song of Solomon. The relationship Trible perceives between the two Scriptures increases the richness of both sections and radically transforms our beliefs about the nature of female-male existence.

The creation of Adam is ambiguous because, in translating Hebrew into English we have translated 'adham as man, and we think naturally of a biological male partly because of the duties prescribed for 'adham in Genesis 3:17-19. However, 'adham is a generic term for humankind. Until the differentiation of female and male (occurring in Genesis 2:21-23) 'adham is basically androgynous: one creature incorporating both sexes. Trible points out that the creation of woman and the concern for the sexuality of the pair occurs last in the story. Whereas some interpreters have judged this order to imply female subordination, Trible sees it as consistent with the priests' account in Genesis 1:27 where the sexes are created simultaneously and readers infer equality.

She makes this assertion by paying attention to the construction of the myth. Both the biblical theologian and the literary critic know that the last may be first. In Genesis 2, woman, Trible argues, may be seen as the culmination or completion of creation, not as an inferior afterthought. In Hebrew literature the main elements of a story often appear at the beginning and at the end of a story. Thus, the creation of man first and woman second in the Genesis 2 account may illustrate a ring composition suggesting completeness and equality.

Trible continues her exegesis by discussing the significance of the creation of woman as helper, a term which has frequently been used to designate inferiority in contemporary culture. According to Trible's interpretation, God is the helper of Israel and as helper he creates and saves.[11] The animals are also helpers but they fail to fulfill completely the needs of 'adham. Thus woman as a helper equal to man is created by God, the helper superior to human beings.

At the creation of woman a different term is used to refer to man as a male sexual being ('ish). Prior to the creation of woman only the term 'adham has been used.

> Only with the specific creation of woman ('ishshah) occurs the first specific term for man as male ('ish). In other words, sexuality is simultaneous for woman and man. The sexes are interrelated and interdependent. Man as male does not precede woman as female but happens concurrently with her. Hence, the first act in Genesis 2 is the creation of androgeny (2:7) and the last is the creation of sexuality (2:23). Male embodies female and female embodies male. The two are neither dichotomies nor duplicates.[12]

Here then we find male and female existing in mutuality and union.

While persons skeptical of Trible's reinterpretation of Genesis 2 may be able to accept hesitantly her different analysis of the ancient text, they often feel compelled to anticipate difficulty in removing the responsibility from woman for the fall. Trible speculates about the reasons that the serpent approaches the woman rather than the man to eat the fruit. The woman is the one who contemplates the tree; she considers its purpose and meaning. She is "both theologian and translator."[13] She knows that the tree is physically as well as emotionally satisfying, and it is the source of wisdom (haskil).

In deciding to eat the fruit of the tree the woman acts independently and decisively. The man, on the other hand, simply follows her action more or less passively, even though he received directly the admonition not to eat of the tree. Both are responsible for their alienation from God and their separation from each other: the woman because she struggled directly with the temptation to disobey and the man because he did not resist her example. What is also particularly interesting in the story, as Trible interprets it, is the portrayal of the two characters. In a culture dominated by man the depiction of both is unusual.

The consequences of the disobedience of both woman and man—judgment by God—must be read as "commentaries on the disastrous effects of their shared disobedience."[14] Until recently we have read the state of separation between woman and man as the inevitable condition of human existence. Instead we now need to consider that the judgments are merely descriptions of human separation—not prescriptions for the female-male relationship.

> Of special concern are the words telling the woman that her husband shall rule over her (3:16). This statement is not license for male supremacy, but rather it is condemnation of that very pattern. Subjugation and supremacy are perversions of creation. Through disobedience the woman has become slave. Her initiative and her freedom vanish. The man is corrupted also, for he has become master, ruling over the one who is his God-given equal. The subordination of female to male signifies their shared sin.[15]

At this point in the story the man names his wife Eve and in the act of naming gains power over her. "The naming itself faults the man for corrupting a relationship of mutuality and equality."[16] By no longer being one with his wife, he treats her as an object, a being unrelated to himself, and he denies her a reciprocal right (shared in love) to name herself with him.

It is a fully functioning imagination that has aided in the above depatriarchalizing and revitalizing of an ancient myth. Through the process we may come closer to the truth of the creation myth and its power in the present. An alive imagination also perceives relationships where others have ignored or failed to see them. Trible has studied the Song of Solomon, a book that has perplexed theologians for centuries. The erotic poetry collected in the Song of Solomon is usually treated principally as an allegory of God's love for Israel or of Christ's love for the church rather than as a description of human love.

What Trible has done is to relate the Song to the Genesis 2 creation story. Through the association of the Yahwist narrative with the poetry of the Song of Solomon we more fully understand union and mutuality between woman and man in a regained Paradise. Through serious reading of the love poetry we ourselves may find clues to the divine intent of the male and female relationship. The garden of Genesis 2, which falls into barrenness in Genesis 3, is reclaimed or recultivated and enlarged in the Song of Solomon.

In both the Genesis and Song gardens there are trees, spices, flowers, water—giving sensuous pleasure to the couples. Animals are present in both gardens; in Genesis they are inferior helpers to humanity, but in the Song they participate metaphorically in the expressions of the lovers. From the woman:

> My beloved is like a gazelle,
> or a young stag . . . (2:9).
>
> his locks are wavy,
> black as a raven (5:11).
>
> His eyes are like doves
> beside springs of water (5:12).[17]

And from the man to describe the woman:

> Behold, you are beautiful, my love,
> > behold, you are beautiful!
> Your eyes are doves
> > behind your veil.
> Your hair is like a flock of goats,
> > moving down the slopes of Gilead.
> Your teeth are like a flock of shorn ewes
> > that have come up from the washing,
> All of which bear twins,
> > and not one among them is bereaved (4:1-2). . . .
>
> Your two breasts are like two fawns,
> > twins of a gazelle,
> > that feed among the lilies (4:5).

In such description we find not only mutual adoration between woman and man but also human identity with nature that no longer suggests a fallen creation, marked by domination and submission, but a renewed garden.

The naming that occurs in both gardens by the nameless couples is dissimilar. In Genesis the naming is an act of domination that, in the human relationship, is a rejection of mutuality. However, in the Song

> authority vanishes, and perversion is unknown, The woman names the man:
> > For your love is better than wine,
> > > your anointing oils are fragrant,
> > Your *name* is oil poured out;
> > > therefore the maidens love you (1:2b-3).
> Her act is wholly fitting and good. Naming is ecstasy, not exercise; it is love, not control. And that love marks a new creation.[18]

The power present in the Song that flows through the paradise and that potentially can transform the fallen garden is the love between the sexes. The Song reveals the mutuality of male and female. As lovers, woman and man alternately pursue one another. "They treat each other with tenderness and respect, for they are sexual lovers, not sexual objects. They neither exploit nor escape sex; they embrace and enjoy it."[19] Sexual love, concrete love, is the redeeming condition for human relationship and the mediator between life and destruction.

In the Song of Solomon there is not a hint of rejection of the material world or of human sexuality. "Love is the meaning of their life, and this love excludes oppression and exploitation. It knows the goodness of sex and hence it knows not sexism."[20] To know this kind of love requires the power of imagination, the ability to hold in one's mind and heart the ever-changing whole being of the beloved. The cultivation of the imagination and our mythic capacities allows us to perceive our identification with our individual pasts as well as a corporate human history and to be informed by the truth expressed in myth.

What Phyllis Trible has done as a biblical scholar we who are not such scholars cannot do. But her scholarly efforts of scriptural reinterpretation combined with her ability to seek truth in ancient myth paves the way toward a renamed garden in the present. With our own awakened imaginations we can continue renaming the garden as we refuse to live with limited vision and unquestioning, inactive minds. Accepting the fallen creation, marked by alienation and separation, makes growth toward wholeness through love impossible. The vision of what can be, rooted in concrete experiences and expressions of our mutual sexuality, brings wholeness in a renamed garden into being.

If the marks of the renamed garden are: affirmation of sexuality rather than rejection of it, mutuality between the sexes rather than independence and dependence, fluidity of roles rather than role stereotyping, wholeness of being rather than compartmentalization, and relationship with and delight in nature rather than exploitation of nature—then what can we do with those myths that seem to support a fallen creation and that keep us trapped in separation?

Myths that seem narrowly to circumscribe life or make rigid prescriptions for behavior, I assert, are controlled myths; that is, they are literalized and used as prescriptive cudgels rather than symbolic representations to ease one's passage through life. The myths are not faulty; they contain their own aspects of truth. What is faulty is our manipulation of them. Myths are by nature expansive in that they urge us to move into life, to confront the unknown, to hold faith in the midst of despair, to act with courage in the face of fear.

When myths are used to shield us from life, to separate us into inferior and superior races, to draw us into passivity, they become tools of oppression. To the extent that we actively respond to existing myths and contribute our own insights to the interpretation of existing myths, we are not likely to be entrapped by restrictive "myths."

Three classic myths about the nature of woman, discussed in detail by Simone de Beauvoir, illustrate ways in which myth can become restrictive: (1) the myth of the "eternal feminine," (2) the myth of "woman as other," and (3) the myth of "feminine mystery."

All three of these myths are rooted in the assumption that woman and man are fixed, antagonistic entities. There is no longer mutuality or reciprocity suggested in them. Their grip on us is strong because some psychoanalytic work, such as that of Sigmund Freud, has contributed to the fixedness of sexual nature, and thus has tended to literalize the myth that was originally a symbolic description of woman.

In the modern mind the "eternal feminine" myth implies that biological nature influences distinctly all other aspects of personality. It is used to describe complex, variable individuals *in toto* by ascribing to them static, unvarying, and eternal qualities usually associated with fecundity. Therefore, at one time women may be instructed by the "eternal feminine" myth that they are pure, saintly mothers, beings of light; at another time or in another context they are described *en masse* as ruthless stepmothers, as praying mantises, creatures of darkness. Regardless of the particular emphasis, light or dark, the function of the myth of the "eternal feminine" is to attribute to all females a composite, generalized nature without attention to or respect for specific departures from the mythic nature.

For many contemporary women being persons is not, as it may have been in earlier times, largely dependent on the

biologically maternal capacity; therefore, they find themselves in conflict with a powerful myth of the society that
prompts women to find total fulfillment in procreation. For
example, one woman I have known well for about ten years
reported her struggle as a young woman to develop maternal
instincts which were authentically secondary to her artistic
and computive interests and skills.

> Much of my adolescent life I deeply believed I was not only an ab-
> normal youth, but I feared I was a sexually frigid female. These con-
> cerns were not just harbored inside me, but I was told by psy-
> chologists that I was frigid, a maladjusted female who would never
> give birth to a child and would likely find heterosexual relations dif-
> ficult if not repulsive.

Today this woman has a brilliant daughter and is herself a
self-aware, straightforward person whose interests range
beyond and yet include the care of her child.

Can there be any truth in a myth that restricts women in
the way the "eternal feminine" myth seems to have done to
women repeatedly? Surely to expect a woman to be only a
biologically productive human being is to deny her wholeness. How specious our reasoning if we assume that fertility
is a quality relegated only to women! The myth of the "eternal feminine" demands broader application.

Both women and men must come to cherish the
qualities of fruitfulness and nourishment; they must learn,
perhaps from the kernel of truth in the myth itself, their joint
opportunity to be caretaker-parents of the human family.
Would not our neighborhoods be transformed places if the
men as well as the women accepted the call to be nurturers
one to another, to translate the so-called feminine qualities
into everyday action? As women we must reject the limiting
aspects of the myth but accept and teach a wider interpretation of it.

The universalization of a myth is another way of
manipulating and distorting it. A myth universalized limits
the development of more relevant, individual myths or dis-
regards other myths already functioning within the same or
different cultures. To the extent that women squeeze them-

selves into the restrictive "eternal feminine" mold, the effect of this universalized myth is to alienate individual women from their inner lives and personal myths.

The problem of universalization can be illustrated further by the research of Margaret Mead. Her study of three primitive societies reveals that

> . . . while every culture has in some way institutionalized the roles of men and women, it has not necessarily been in terms of contrast between the prescribed personalities of the two sexes, nor in terms of dominance or submission . . . no culture has failed to seize upon the conspicuous facts of age and sex in some way, whether it be the convention of one Philippine tribe that no man can keep a secret, the Manus assumption that only men enjoy playing with babies, the Toda prescription of almost all domestic work as too sacred for women, or the Arapesh insistence that women's heads are stronger than men's.[21]

With each of these examples from tribal groups we find our own cultural myths about the nature of women and men at variance; yet through our universalized myths we prescribe for all others as well as ourselves. Primitive people seem to be somewhat more sophisticated than we are about not universalizing their myths or beliefs.

> . . . they know that the gods, the food habits, and the marriage customs of the next tribe differ from those of their own people, and do not insist that one form is true or natural while the other is false or unnatural . . . they often know that the temperamental proclivities which they regard as natural for men or for women differ from the natural temperaments of the men and women among their neighbors.[22]

Because we cannot know absolutely what is the genuine nature of individuals, we must avoid literalizing and universalizing a myth that grew from a specific set of circumstances and from people whose lives may have differed somewhat from our own.

The myth of the "woman as other" has not only social acceptability but also a long history of religious sanction. For Jews and Christians at least, the roots of the myth of "woman as other" are found in patriarchal interpretations of Genesis 2. As traditionally presented, the Genesis 2 narrative depicts woman created from the side of Adam; she is "other," different from man, sometimes helpmate and sometimes seductress. But in most interpretations she is overagainst man, in tension with him but without reciprocity.

To view woman as "other" is to put her out of reach as a functioning, influencing person. Woman as "other," whether "other" is understood as spirit or as sexual temptress, is stripped of her sexuality and has had her personhood severed. The myth of "woman as other" isolates women from humanity and associates a set of "pure" characteristics to females alone. Such a belief about woman makes interchange and intercourse between a woman and a man nearly impossible. " . . . the 'pure' male and the 'pure' female have nothing in common and no means of communication with each other."[23] For relationship to exist between a woman and a man there must be reciprocity, interdependence, and equality.

> The idea of equality in the sacred sphere has often been taken to mean the disappearance of sexuality, since St. Paul said that in Christ there is neither male nor female, and Jesus said that in heaven there is neither marriage nor giving in marriage. But the latter remark is only to say that heaven, the sacred sphere, stands above the social institutions of the profane sphere. Conversely, the secular notion of sexual equality is one that merely permits women to behave like men, and the two parodies, the Churchly and the secular, are equally sexless rather than sexually equal. Sexual equality should properly mean sexual fulfillment, the woman realizing her masculinity through man, and the man realizing his femininity through woman.[24]

Trible's reinterpretation of Genesis 2 contrasts with the popular understanding of the myth of "woman as other." Instead of being in tension with man, woman is completer of and completed in relationship with man. Mutuality and equality, not distinct separation and isolation, are the divine qualities of human relationship.

The third myth, the myth of "feminine mystery," illustrates what occurs when myth is severed from the experiential dimension of life and is transferred to idea. Certainly in every human being there exists the element of mystery. Thank God for that. But that mystery must always be perused in the particular, not as an abstraction to be assigned, as a deficiency in nature, to a whole sex. No doubt the notion of "feminine mystery" was tied originally to specific cultural experience and concrete persons, but again as we have increased our knowledge of human physiology, psychology, sociology, and anthropology we are not so overwhelmed by such one-time physiologic mysteries as the female menses, pregnancy, or childbirth.

Simone de Beauvoir asserts that the development of the idea of "feminine mystery" was designed by men who have refused to relate to individual, variable women. Instead of genuine human encounter, the notion of "feminine mystery" permits escape from relationships of dignity and equality. Such a myth can readily gain stature as idea or "fact" in a culture in which paternalism is rooted in dualism and in which relationships are defined by dominance or submission and over-againstness. Our dualistic culture has forced us to divide, to oppose, and to polarize not only our life experiences but, more sadly, our human unity.

What, we may ask, can we do to recover our mythic capacities? And how can we see truth where we have learned to expect illusion or deception? Two myths, closely related to the three above, bear reexamination. In reexamining the myths we may rediscover some capacities of the imagination that enable us to see truth in the myths that we are prone to reject. The myth of the self-sacrificial nature of the female and the myth of the female's more highly developed spiritual nature have been instrumental in shaping the consciences and life-choices of most Christian women. Both myths are currently under attack, particularly by feminists. Again, because culturally we have literalized the myths and have used them as prescriptions for women, we are now angrily repudiating them as lies.

If myth arises out of human experience then it should be easy to see that a myth about the self-sacrificing nature of females might have sprung from observation of the response of a woman to her child. Running to feed, to protect, to nurture the child, a woman's behavior is serving, self-sacrificing in that moment. One can, I trust, imagine a positive response to such a scene. The nurture of life arouses compassion in healthy souls, regardless of the sex of the nurturer.

By allowing the myth of self-sacrifice to move them into passivity, women have given control for their lives to something or someone outside themselves. In so doing, women have permitted men to be cut off from their own sacrificial, nurturant nature. Now, with dysfunctioning imaginations, we are in the questionable position of wholeheartedly rejecting the value of conscious, chosen self-sacrifice and of embracing the cultural myths that undergird human self-centeredness, aggressiveness, and acquisitiveness.

What the admittedly distorted myth of the self-sacrificial nature of females did contribute to the culture was an acceptable ground for nurture and service. As we women reject that aspect of human, not solely female, nature we run the risk of replacing it with another controlled myth: that healthy human beings are predominantly self-interested, goal-oriented, and competitive. Somewhere there must be reunion with the poles of our nature. Such reunion can only occur through the aid of an alive imagination that constantly interprets and shapes myth.

Like the self-sacrificial myth, the myth of a highly developed spiritual nature in females may have arisen from observation of oppressed women who dealt with that oppression through spiritual meditation. Regardless of its roots, it has been under the control of the powerful in the culture, those who see social leadership and decision-making as the nitty-gritty realities that have little to do with the spirit. They have kept females from participating in the guidance of the affairs of state at the same time they have justified their own control of those affairs by assigning women to a spiritual sphere of activity. When our mythic capacities awaken we can reject the manipulation and distortion and open the whole spectrum of human experiences to all human beings.

The only ways for us to reclaim our mythic capacities, and thereby to find myth again a helpful avenue to move through life and to make contact with other human beings, are to trust our experiences and to accept our own Abrahamic call to wander away from those messages that sever our personal wholeness and separate us from one another. In order for us even to begin such a journey, supported by our imaginations and conducted for self-discovery, human preservation and reunion, we must affirm with Don Quixote that the highest goods are the integrity and sanctity of each life and a vision of the world not simply as it is but as it ought to be. Jesus' life seems to bear testimony to these two ends. Having affirmed these ends, we can proceed to create and to use our personal myths to explore our own lives and our relationship to the world.

Into My Own

Read the Genesis accounts of creation anew with Trible's guides in mind.
Read the Song of Solomon as beautiful love poetry.
Reread any of the fairy tales you read as a child. Can you recall what they
meant to you as a child? What do you find in them now?

Chapter 4.

I AM: THE IMPORTANCE
OF NAMING

The universe resounds with the joyful cry "I am."—Scriabin

Shortly after the birth of our first child I found myself in the social company of some women and men who were well known to me. These were people with whom I had had, over several years, pleasant discussions on a wide range of subjects. As I moved from conversation to conversation that evening the topic under discussion in each group was dropped when I entered. The question posed upon my entry was, "Well, how is the baby?" I appreciated their interest. What distressed me was the implicit assumption that now that my role had somehow changed so would my interests and the very person I was.

The problem illustrated by this example is the recurring one of "naming." How shall I "name" myself to others? How do others "name" me? For many of us, "naming" has become a perfunctory obligation we meet with social correctness by answering identity questions with ritualistic replies. "I am Sarah Jean Smith of Yonkers, New York."

For others, "naming" is done for us by the various roles we are called upon to play. "I am a teacher, a homemaker, a doctor, the wife of, or the mother of, or the employee of." We all name our sense of place—our homes, our jobs, our cities, and our nations; we name our organizational affiliations and our possessions, all of which tell us and others who we are.

Such naming is described by Eric Berne, Thomas Harris, and other transactional analysts as rituals and pastimes. They help us stay in contact with one another, but what we learn through this conventional communication, we would probably agree, is limited. Customarily understood as a static procedure of affixing labels to objects and ascribing inflexible characteristics to people, naming encourages us to reduce human lives to predictability and changelessness. Yet it is with this kind of naming that most of us are tempted to spend most of our lives. We accept static naming for our brief, superficial social encounters. But what about those relationships in which we have greater opportunity to know and to be known? How do we name, or define, ourselves in our more prolonged encounters and more intimate relationships?

The journey to self-knowledge begins by reflectively and with delight taking oneself seriously. What things do I particularly like? What things do I strongly hate? What are my greatest fears? What are my highest ambitions or dreams? What do I love most to do, or feel most capable of doing? What qualities in other people do I most seek out? What characteristics in others frighten or threaten me? Is there anything for the sake of which I would die?

We cannot ask these kinds of questions without becoming aware of our own complicated natures. From such probing we will soon learn the further limitations of "naming" ourselves and others as we are conventionally expected to do.

If naming is not to be understood as a onetime act, a dependence upon stereotypes and labels, how shall we describe it? Naming, in the sense that I wish to use it throughout this book, results from a recurring experience of being and is foremost a process of thought; it is a reflective approach to oneself and the world, the end of which is the discovery and disclosure of our ever-changing, inner, authentic selves. This kind of naming gives rebirth to our mythic and faith capacities. We find clues in the Old Testament to the understanding of naming as the most important psychological function of life.

For Yahweh the act of creation was simultaneously an act of naming. The "names" that Yahweh implanted on "his" creation were not tags but experiences of being that occurred within the hearts of living people. Jeremiah's call to prophesy, for example, was a call *to be,* not simply a request to carry out a task or to function in a role. His sacred mission was rooted in his identity (his name). In Jeremiah 1:5 God speaks, "Before I formed you in the womb I knew you, and before you were born I consecrated you; I appointed you a prophet to the nations." The decisive verbs in this passage give assurance of God's continuing presence with him, and permits him to recognize his chosenness (his unique name).

Abram's call from God is to "Go from your country and your kindred and your father's house to the land that I will show you." (Genesis 12:1). He is to give up his old identity, which is secured by traditional relationships with family and location, and to respond to a new name which God promises him (Genesis 17:5). Abraham's obedient response to God's call rises from an *inner* awareness that he is not free to reject the call. It is as if God created in the being of Abraham the restlessness that could rest only in relationship with God and with the acknowledgment of his new name.

God's creative activity within these people caused them to respond to their names (beings) by becoming namers of the world; they did not passively receive a label that neatly defined them. Through the Being-ness of God they grew to understand themselves as beings that were called, simply by their holy creation, to live connected with every living being. In that connection with Yahweh, who described "himself" in Exodus 3:13-14 as "I am," and with all other forms of being, they were able to know, and thereby name, themselves. Without that dynamic experience of being, of feeling the presence of God within them, they could not know themselves fully. The experience of Jeremiah and of Abraham is the promise for all living beings, though we may be contemporarily out of earshot of that promise.

For us in our own day, once we have categorized one another and the birds of the air and the fish of the sea, there is, we think, nothing left to do except to absorb the sun or the rain and to be buffeted by various winds. This cataloguing of living beings leads us to respond to the world as a dead place and to ourselves as mummies. In contrast, dynamic naming requires us to expect the unexpected, to hear within ourselves new calls, to see new visions, to understand anew old words, to accept change as God's gift for growth.

The two major goals of naming with which we are concerned here are self-knowledge and dialogue. Again an Old Testament usage of naming is instructive. To name is to know in the way that a woman and a man know themselves and one another in mutual sexual intimacy. To be self-aware one must be continuously attentive to her changing feelings, her ideas, her responses. She must, figuratively speaking, have intercourse with her own being. The variations, the newness she discovers, she must then speak to the world around her through her words and actions.

The second goal of naming, inseparable from the first, is to make dialogue possible. To achieve this end, naming is used as the means through which one enters into dialogue. The kind of dialogue I am discussing is clearly more than an exchange of agreed-upon symbols that foster conversation. It is best described as a meeting of meanings.[1] In terms used by transactional analysts it is the experience of intimacy with another human being.

Naming, then, is perhaps the essential task of living. Unlike other species of life, the human being has the capacity for reflection upon itself and deliberate action outward toward the world. Reflection and action make naming in the sense of knowing possible. To name is to come to terms with, to know oneself and one's world, including other human beings. Not to name is not to know.

Do all people possess equally the capacity to name their experiences? How does one keep alive that capacity? How is the capacity lost? And how can it be regained?

Every human being born into the world seeks instinctively to learn her personal dimensions in relationship to the vast dimensions of the world. From birth one acts upon the world and is acted upon. With the progressive development of thought and verbalization one gains further tools through which to encounter the world.

These natural and developed capacities to communicate outwardly and, simultaneously, inwardly are kept alive so long as one is able to maintain a view of oneself as subject as well as object. When you understand yourself as a subject-object, you know that you are *both* an actor, thinker, creator (subject) and a receiver of others' actions (object). You are a whole being grounded, as were Abraham and Jeremiah, in the great "I am." Whenever you no longer are able to trust yourself as capable of acting for yourself or when you permit yourself to be limited by others as their object, then you have lost your ability to engage in naming.

One's freedom to name is inevitably in tension with the restrictive naming done by others, but the desired dialogue, one goal of naming, occurs when whole people meet to name the world together. Dialogue cannot occur between those who choose to name and those who do not wish to name.[2] The result of not naming is that one is named only as an object of others, not as a subject-object, whole being.

The ability to name can be lost by giving up one's right to name for another goal. One such goal may be a comfortable, though misleading, security that grows from letting others tell us who we are. Another way to deny the self as subject is to place a higher priority on social customs than on independent thought and action. By believing that it is better to have domestic peace (either in the home or in the society) than personal wholeness, one may reject oneself as namer. Lost or denied ability to define one's world is recovered by getting in touch with oneself as a vital whole being again. How might one do that?

Joseph Campbell, author of *The Masks of God,* was asked in an interview whether one discovers personhood through interaction and relationship with a group or by some individual quest made in solitude. His response was that one finds herself or himself only as she or he is willing to go alone on paths no one else has taken before her or him because, in fact, no two human beings can ever make the same journey inward. The territory is always varied. Then, Campbell was asked, where may one find guidance for such a journey toward self-knowledge? To this Campbell replied:

> . . . follow your own bliss. This involves analysis, watching yourself and seeing where the real deep bliss is—not the quick little excitement, but the real, deep life-fulfilling bliss.[3]

As one continually makes this kind of journey one also is able to enter into dialogue with the world. Is this startling advice in a group-oriented age? It seems to suggest isolation out of which dialogue would be impossible. What instead Campbell may be suggesting is that there can be no dialogue, no relationship of whole people, until you know yourself as a unique whole seeking dialogue that is complementary with other whole beings. Without the private inward quest we remain where many people are today—looking for definition, as objects, from those around them.

Large numbers of human beings in our society are not engaged in the dynamic act of naming themselves and their worlds. The fact that one possesses the *tool* with which to speak (the word) does not necessarily mean that he or she has accepted or maintained the *right* to speak that word, whatever it may be. Anyone who is oppressed, and acquiesces in that oppression, by another human being or an inflexible and unjust social order, has lost the ability to name the world. The ability to name, to act as a subject on the world is not necessarily given up with a violent show of resistance. More often it disappears quietly, almost unknowingly, because the potential subject has found a kind of security in the limits of the prescription placed on her or him from without.

The poor in any society are largely at the mercy of the rich. They are denied economic participation; and where economic power is an unwritten prerequisite for political, social, and educational participation, the poor are alienated from the groups which are responsible for shaping a society. The poor have their own ways of naming the world, and many individuals living in poverty may have strong self-concepts. However, when they are excluded from interaction with the larger society and have their approaches to the world and human relationships ignored or devalued, they are not permitted to enter dialogue with the world as a whole. It follows that even those with resilient self-concepts cannot tolerate this lack of involvement as a subject indefinitely. Sooner or later they believe themselves to be the objects upon which naming and acting occur, and they surrender their ability to be and to name who they are.

The perennially ridiculed English class is, sadly, often a place where powerless students give up their right to name the world. We, and literate society in general, expect English teachers to protect acceptable language usage and to reeducate the poor and minority groups whose language patterns fall short of the so-called ideal. Until recently this expectation, taken seriously by most institutions of higher education preparing English teachers, negatively discriminated against the life experiences of large segments of the American citizenry and deprived them of their most essential instrument of self-knowledge and self-expression: human language. For years black Americans have been told that their language patterns are incorrect; the unarticulated message was received clearly by this group of Americans. It was, of course, that their approach to and understanding of their own experience and the nature of the world were inferior. How are you to name yourself when denied your authentic voice?

I have known many young people who, at the height of

their physical vitality and at the period in their lives when their intellectual curiosity should have been grappling with their worlds, said to me, "I didn't say nothing 'cause I can't say things the right way." Such a response soon grows into silence and ultimately to indifference. Repeatedly we have alienated human beings from themselves and the world by usurping their right to name, and, simultaneously, their capacity to think and to respond spontaneously. Fortunately for all of us, we are now becoming enlightened enough to examine varying language structures and patterns within English and to permit legitimacy for that variety. By so doing we also give value to variety in human experiences.

Women make up another group of people who have been led into what Paulo Freire, a Brazilian educator, has termed the "culture of silence" of the dispossessed.[4] Freire undertakes to analyze the South American peasants who by economic, political, and social domination have been turned into silent chambers. The kind of domination experienced by most American women is primarily psychological domination created by prescriptive defining of them. Women have learned characteristics of submission from the paternalistic culture that values what it labels "masculine" qualities of independence, rationality, competitiveness, and strength.

The gentle qualities of sensitivity, intuition, dependence, weakness, and cooperation have been named for females not necessarily as a dynamic description of live women but as a way the female segment of the population can be grasped. As individual women, who may not by nature or choice fit these prescriptions or possess these qualities alone, attempt to make such definitions fit, they unavoidably lose their selves as actors, as subjects that define the world and themselves. Consequently, you and I may have become quiet chambers unable to share who we are authentically.

Why view females as having been denied or as having surrendered their power of naming more so than males? To the extent that *any* human being limits himself or herself to the prescriptions of others and responds only as a predictable object in the service of namers, he or she has been dehumanized. Males, simply because the qualities ascribed to them over generations and sanctioned by the Judeo-Christian heritage, have been celebrated and dominant in Western culture, have had encouragements to keep alive their capacity for naming, albeit that capacity turns into domination or manipulation when deprived of the intuitive qualities of compassion and gentleness. According to social prescription, men are to be the namers and the actors. The common notion of woman as the other half of man, the non-rational part, submissive to his authority, suggests her inevitable dehumanization, and, if we think clearly, his as well.

How can we know that women have given up or been tempted to give up their call to participate in naming themselves and the world? A woman wrote to me in the early stages of my work on this book to share an interesting story about the expectations others had of her as a young female. When she was about three and a half or four years old, she regularly played with a group of community children. One day some in the gang suggested they take a walk. They started out directionless. My friend reports that she suggested they all go to her father's office, which was several blocks away, and then to the church, which was another block farther. They were gone from home about an hour. When they returned, she reported, her mother was furious with "those boys" because they had taken the little girl away. The expectation was clearly that little women would not be so curious or disobedient or spontaneous as to lead their group to places that are important to them. Little boys are expected to be those things.

Perhaps the time when women subtly receive the greatest pressure to become "silent chambers" is during adolescence. I remember almost with visual clarity a day around age fourteen when I decided that if I wanted to be a "popular" female I would have to give up some intellectual interests or at least be quiet about them around young men. A friend I have had since high school stated her experiences in this way:

"By my peers, I was made to see that 'smart' girls who answered questions in class where shunned by boys, and so I began to play dumb with the result that I had dates but felt secretly superior to many of them. I do feel that a hostility towards men and the unfairness of society began then. I learned to 'shut up.' Now, I feel the need to express myself as I once knew how, but I no longer have the tools at hand with which to do it. I feel the need to relate to men on an intellectual level, but my hostility becomes a barrier. I want to find a way to enter into the working world, but my previous choices and lack of training prohibit me."

These kinds of dilemmas do not, unfortunately, belong only to the 1950s and 60s. Despite the consciousness raising that has gone on throughout the culture in the past ten years about sex role stereotyping, young adults continue to struggle to know themselves and to relate themselves authentically to one another. Last spring on a small college campus my husband and I talked with about thirty young people about these issues. Many young men admitted that they had trouble listening to women's ideas; others confessed that thinking of the sexual aspects of a woman always seems predominant in a male/female relationship. Some of the women expressed frustration at their own inability to overcome their silence when around men. Others talked about feeling guilty when they were academically more successful than their male counterparts. All of them wanted to break through these kinds of barriers that keep people from being whole and meeting freely.

How we identify ourselves, how we feel about ourselves depends in great part on how our parents knew themselves and helped us to know ourselves. Those of us who are parents now give to our children our understanding of who we are and of whose call is upon our lives. We also tell them in countless ways who they are and show them faith or despair in their beings. We teach them either to accept that of God in themselves and to become namers of the world or to reject that gift and become silent chambers shaped by external forces. Two very different stories illustrate this point.

I met a young woman years ago and simultaneously learned to know her family. Not until three years ago did I hear her story about her mother's significance in her life

When she wrote to me then she began by quoting a passage from Robin Morgan's book *Sisterhood Is Powerful* that summed up her own feelings about the definitions she had received from others about being female. Morgan writes:

> . . . having your first real human talk with your mother and being told all about her old hopes and lost ambitions, and how you can't fight it, and that's just the way it is: life, sex, men, the works—and loving her and hating her for having been so beaten down.[5]

Then my friend continued.

> "Well, I remember the very talk described in those words with *my* mother about how she wanted to be a doctor above all else and then this happened and then this happened and . . . I remember remembering at that time the stationery we as kids had found under her bed even years after our move from the city to our small town home, stationery printed up for a doll hospital in the city. I remember remembering how sad I felt thinking that even the substitute hadn't worked out. Then I remember thinking of all the years between then and this very talk, the years of frustrated attempts to live out her creativity within the home, then within the framework of an elementary classroom, all the time becoming less able to come across as mother to her own children and all the time coming up with the coverall phrase ' . . . out of loyalty to your father' or 'well, your father is the head of this household. . . ,' never telling us in so many words that the whole thing was a drag; in fact, trying from our earliest years on to play down any real interest in the creative side of things. To be 'well-practiced but not creative' seemed to be the aim of her molding. And I remember the confused feeling after that talk, marveling on the one hand about this, our first mother-daughter talk with mother spilling out in some sort of honesty, but on the other hand, recoiling from the realization that I wanted to hate her for passing up her own life 'out of loyalty for my father' no matter what the circumstances may have been, for thereby messing up her own psyche in such a way as to affect me and the course my life might be taking as a result; for perhaps disliking—or certainly at least distrusting—me because I would not see the necessity of her way.
>
> "Then I thought of my daughter Ann Elise. I realized that I have only gone halfway in preventing the same mistake from being carried on. I realized that although I think of her in terms of a mother sometimes, that's not the main way I picture her into the future. I picture her as fulfilled in a way that my mother was not and in the way that I was not raised to be. I see in her a very intelligent, bright, personality-full child and project these characteristics onto her in the future, to be fit out with whatever it is specifically she decides to do.

But I do picture her doing something beyond mothering. From there it wasn't far to realize that, as an example, I am setting up perhaps the shell of this life, the shell of fulfillment. That is, I am in a position that I must work. I am thankful for that, having known always that, normal or not, I was not cut out to be a twenty-four-hour housewife and/or mother. Therefore, I have geared the rest of my life toward the successful handling of career and motherhood and have enjoyed the setup of that situation. The shell is there. But I have not really faced the question of fulfillment. I don't *ever* want Ann Elise to have 'to love and/or hate me for having been beaten down.'"

A musician, mother, and church executive described a contrasting experience of identity-shaping. From both her parents she learned what wholeness meant. She identified with her father's deep Christian commitment and shared his love of study, reading, and reflection of God's love manifested in nature. Her mother possessed those qualities as well and, in addition, was enthusiastic about sports, pole vaulting and basketball in particular. My friend remembers traveling with her parents, who both played on teams, and rooting for them. "This helped me to know that women are just as able as men when they pursue their own interests," observes my friend.

This mother defied any stereotype of a stay-at-home mousey woman. In church and community affairs both parents were active. When my friend's mother had special jobs to do and did not have time for all the things expected of her, she asked or hired someone else to help her. "Her willingness to get help," reports my friend, "taught me unconsciously that one person cannot be and do all the things a typical wife-mother is supposed to do if she is unselfishly to give any time to others outside her four walls."

What these stories illustrate are two possible responses to one's life. Though here they both describe women's responses, they could as easily characterize men's reactions. In the first response the mother described chose conformity or adjustment to an assumed set of role prescriptions with a resultant frustration. In the second, the woman chose to stay attentive to herself as much as to the expectations of those around her. We all live with the perpetual pressure to conform or fit in, and we are often misled to place, for ourselves and for our children, acceptability ahead of selfawareness and integrity

Though adjustment to a social norm may be necessary and in some instances highly desirable, one dare not confuse social adaptation with personhood. While the two may occur together, they are sometimes mutually exclusive. To adjust to what already exists or is prescribed for us may seem to be easier and more expedient in the short run but may, in the longer view, require significant sacrifices of our inner beings. To know oneself and to hold a vision of life lived authentically by all people demands much of our imaginations.

How do we begin to perceive ourselves and the world imaginatively? What might be *our* Don Quixote acts essential for our own selfhood? What sallies might we undertake to transform ourselves?

An avocational musician, with a cultivated appreciation of Mozart, Beethoven, Brahms, and Stravinsky symphonies, learned some new things about her being from the folkprotest songs of the 1960s. As she listened to some of the songs, she realized that she was simultaneously becoming more alert to social/political questions. Since then she has read and discussed much more news analysis and commentary and has related to some political action groups. Two recent gift recordings, one of classical guitar and the other of mandolin music, produced a moment of recognition for her.

"I suddenly realized through these two single instruments something about who I am that I never quite understood or accepted before. I am a solitary person; that is, I like to be alone, and I think I care about other alone people—people caught in poverty, children orphaned by wars or unwanted, elderly people who are lonely. The folk song, the guitar, the mandolin express solitariness, a kind of closeness between music and an individual. For some reason my love for the symphony played by a full crashing orchestra seems distant now as an authentic expression of myself."

As we begin to pay attention to our interests in our waking consciousness, we may also find our dreams becoming unusually fertile ground for discovering who we are, what we fear, what aspirations we have.

A loving woman who has been involved in her church for sixty years and whose principal goal in life has been to serve others became confused by a dream that she had during a time of stress in her life as a public schoolteacher. My friend is a conscientious teacher; the intensity of her concern for her students has often made her anxious, exacerbating a mild heart condition. When required by her physician to remain home from her job for several weeks of complete rest, she spent a great amount of time thinking about her class and anticipating her return to the students. She briefly considered terminating her career but decided she wanted to continue and would, if the doctor agreed.

Days later, before returning to her job, she reports that she dreamed she was in her classroom near the end of a day working energetically with a few students. They seemed to demand increasing help and attention, and she needed to break away for an appointment with the doctor. She says she could feel her frustration mount during the dream as she tried to leave to see the doctor, realizing somehow that she had to get to him. Waking from the dream she was exhausted, confused, and nervous.

The point in relating this incident is not principally to do dream analysis but to alert us to information about ourselves that we can receive only from our dreaming. If nothing more, my friend and I agree, her dream heightened her awareness of struggle and ambivalence about her teaching situation. It may also have been a means of communicating the psychological and physical necessity for self-attention rather than continued exhausting concern with the needs of others.

Our imaginations lead us to our fears and our unverbalized longings. But instead of being panicked by them, the active imagination can transform the incapacitation that accompanies repressed fears into energy for self-understanding. By way of myth we are able to act out our longings or express our fears verbally.

A woman I shall call Rita remembers herself as a painfully shy child who ached to laugh and dance freely with other children. She has said,

> "Perhaps you can imagine, or maybe even remember, how it feels when you're ridiculed because your hair is straight and your nose is large or your dress is the same one you wore the day before. Early I internalized the notion, which I at that time thought was inflicted on me from the outside, that I was common, possessing no talent, and dull. Fortunately, I had an imagination. I say fortunately even though I was scared sometimes by the hours I spent in a variety of fantasy worlds by myself. However, it was in my private world that I could become who I thought I was. What happened within my imagination was that I created myths that were expressive of my inner longings and hopes. They were, in some cases, highly elaborate myths about my personal beginning and purpose, not, I suspect, unrelated to creation myths of children through the ages. Through the use of the imagination, I was able to create a putative reality and then to make that reality a part of me. I very much wanted to be a great organist. In my private, inner world I was that. But the wish did not rest complacently in my imagination. Instead, the dream, accompanied by a conscious choice to practice, helped me to lose myself for hours in a deserted sanctuary at an organ console. In some mysterious way the power of the organ swollen to its capacity with sound merged the putative reality and the present reality, and in those moments I was changing myself from a shivering human being into one who finally has some marginal sense of what it means to feel whole."

Is this close to what Don Quixote meant when he wrote, "I know who I am and may become if I choose"? Released within oneself to be herself, one finds sharing her inner being with others less threatening.

If it is true, as some people assert, that creation of a more humane world is hindered only by the limitations of human imagination, then it seems to follow that our own capacities for personal being are limited correspondingly to the extent that we deny our imaginations. In our imaginations rests the point from which faith rises up to accept God's claim on our lives. As we acknowledge God's being within our beings, we are choosing to follow, with Abraham and Jeremiah and Moses and Jesus, the call to wander into a new land. We choose to reject the oppressions, stereotypes, rigid expectations, and fears of the old land.

Throughout the Old Testament the basic marks of a chosen person were the integrity and authenticity of being that relationship with God afforded. A woman who is named by God and chooses *to be* expands her boundaries and potentially transforms, through her own authenticity, everything she touches. She comes to know her being as called forth from the very ground of Being and with that sacred realization shouts "I am" with every breath.

Into My Own

Read Genesis 12, about God's calling of Abram.

Read Genesis 17, about God's covenant with Abram and his name change.

Read Jeremiah 1:4-10, about God's calling of Jeremiah.

Consider the special ways in which you feel called to be a unique human being.

What are the sacred qualities of those closest to you?

Chapter 5.

SELFHOOD AND SERVANTHOOD

In the autonomous self live awareness, spontaneity, and intimacy. —RKJ

Being free, I can choose servanthood. —RKJ

When I talked about the importance of naming on one occasion, a skeptical friend of mine asked, "What's so important about it? Does it really make any difference whether or not I think of myself as a namer?" My hypersensitive nature recoiled, and for several days I thought on her question. What I describe as naming, Erich Fromm talks about as moving toward the healthy or original self. Some of us make that movement through natural growth almost effortlessly; others of us never move toward our own wholeness with ease. Why? What are the conditions that move us toward that end or detain us along the way, fearful and mistrustful? In this chapter I will discuss the namer as an authentic, healthy self; consider some barriers to healthy selfhood; look at Jesus' example concerning selfhood; and, perhaps most importantly, relate selfhood and servanthood.

According to Erich Fromm, every human being chooses one of two responses to life: (1) the development and acceptance of the original self, or (2) the tolerance of a pseudo self. The original self is that one who, having undergone the necessary severing of the primary ties with the world (the mother, the family) in order to achieve independence, embraces freedom for herself or himself and others while simultaneously relating to the world again through her or his own work and love. A person becomes one again with " . . . man [human beings], nature, and himself [herself], without giving up the independence and integrity of his [her] individual self."[1]

The healthy self is authentic. One is able to disclose oneself to others unself-consciously; one's feelings are not hidden; one does not pretend to be aloof and uncommitted. The authentic person accepts solitude, seeing herself or himself as a worthy being in creation. She does not panic in her aloneness; he does not clutch others for his security. Finally, she or he is not afraid of *daemons,*[2] those fears, guilts, anxieties that have the potential to disintegrate us. Confronting those, the authentic person, like Job, recognizes the tension in life between good and evil.

Rollo May writes that the demonic is the destructive side of life without which our constructive, benevolent, loving sides could not exist. The writer of Proverbs 8 recognized both the good and evil aspects of life. With wisdom exists also folly, a prostitute. In both the Old and New Testaments good and evil, light and dark exist side by side to show us that out of chaos and disharmony comes the pull toward order and unity. Accepting all these aspects of one's being, the authentic self can only be an original, never a reprint or a copy.

A pseudo self, on the other hand, arises from a fear of freedom and a resistance to independence. Fromm asserts that fear of freedom and individual responsibility to love and to work forces you to give over your independent self to someone or something else. A pseudo self avoids *daemons,* represses both fears and aspirations, cultivates behavior to meet someone else's desires, is unspontaneous. Such a person's feelings spring not from love of oneself, the world, and others, but from calculation and mistrust.

To some extent we are all encouraged to tolerate pseudo selves. Our need for security may mislead us into contrived behavior in order to receive security. For example, I have sometimes refrained from expressing my opinion on a controversial topic because I feared that others, knowing my opinion, might then not accept me. Whenever I have been silent out of fear I come away feeling phony and untrue to my authentic self. All around us advertisers in the culture give us messages that reinforce pseudo selves. If we accept the message, for example, that we are unattractive, hence unworthy, because we do not wear designer fashions, drive late-model cars, or believe a particular ideology, we conform to external expectations, not our inner beings.

Tolerance of pseudo selves arises principally from our confusion between individualism and autonomy. A paradox of American culture is that all our celebration of individualism has produced a high degree of social conformism. How is that possible? Though autonomy and individualism both generally refer to a state of individual freedom, the difference of emphasis between the two may explain why individualism has not produced *inter*dependence of self-directed people but rather dependent conformism of self-centered people.

Individualism is inward-looking. The interests of the individual are paramount; personal success and happiness are its goals. Because individualism is self-serving, one grasps for things or conditions which will enhance or advance the self. Self-serving is competitive, and competition tends not only to produce conformity but more seriously to perpetrate divisiveness and injustice. In individualistic groups or societies there is little sense of human solidarity. Two Hebrew words, *mishpat* and *sedequah,* in the Old Testament show us the kind of relationship Yahweh desired for the Israelite people. *Mishpat,* translated solidarity, and *sedequah,* translated integrity, reveal the unity or wholeness God intended and Jesus described for all humanity. Any group or social system that does not extend solidarity and integrity to all human beings cannot be in harmony with God.

Autonomy implies independence and self-direction but the emphasis, as elaborated by Fromm in *Escape From Freedom,* seems to be on integration between the self and the external world rather than on self-gratification and competitiveness. The autonomous person assumes responsibility not only for herself or himself but joins with others to share a larger corporate responsibility for the community or world. Self-aggrandizement is not the goal of autonomy, but relating to others through love and work is.

The sense of being one with others, that solidarity promotes, encourages individuals to be autonomous. When an experience of solidarity is missing, people learn mistrust and fear. They are forced to protect themselves alone through means that further separate them from their authentic natures and from one another. Such means might be categorized as barriers to autonomy. Four major barriers that require only short discussion here are: (1) a confusion between identity and role; (2) a denial or restriction of free choice from within or without; (3) the pursuit of stereotyped goals or values; (4) a sense of powerlessness that makes one misuse power.

First, the confusion between identity and role occurs most obviously in adolescence. Two marks that suggest that the confusion does not necessarily pass with adolescence have been offered by Erik Erikson. People who confuse identity and role tend to over-identify with heroes and with popular crowds; they also often display an ideological outlook that seeks affirmation from their peers and is reinforced by various rituals that define what is evil or unacceptable.

The confusion between role and identity is most clearly seen in women. A case in point. Many women over several years have reported to me that the major role they are expected to play in church life is "detail attendant." One bright woman in particular said that on committees her ideas often go unheard; she speaks them and they drop. But when there is any mundane detail work like telephoning or typing or transcribing minutes she is expected to do that immediately. Her identity is obviously bypassed. People who ignore their own identities or have them ignored over a period of time soon begin to look outside themselves for definition. They may take on the style, perhaps, or the values or beliefs of some hero or crowd and give up the quest for their own authentic identity.

The motherhood role is one that is attached to most women. In an attempt to conform to that role women have rallied around various rituals of motherhood—buying the "right" kinds of toothpaste and shoes, providing toys that are competitive with the ones other children have, teaching children to read or not to read before going to school—depending on the latest theory. So busy with squeezing into the motherhood mold, we often neglect our unique thoughts and desires, even thoughts about how to rear our children.

The denial or restriction of free choice from within or without, a second barrier to autonomy, affects women in particular. Such a limitation eventually leads to personal impotence. Many women report giving up personal goals in order to help a husband and/or children achieve their personal goals. These same women, particularly the ones who have reached middle-age, report almost paralyzing uncertainty now about their genuine interests. Not only have many of them lost some of their skills but more sadly they face the dilemma: What is it I really want to do, now that my choices are no longer dictated by my environment and my family?

In the very intimate relationship between the sexes, a female's autonomy is restrained by the teachings of the society. Many women have revealed the kind of counseling they received prior to marriage, counseling often conducted by exclusively male clergy of the church or by mothers whose own marital relationships were shaped by similar admonition. These women reported that they were instructed that a woman's sole responsibility is to satisfy her husband and never to refuse his sexual desires, regardless of what her own needs might be.

My basic concern with such instruction is not primarily that a woman should desire to satisfy a man (*and* vice versa) but that the emphasis seems to be on rejecting one's own needs, one's own desires, one's own self so that she can supposedly better serve her husband without the so-called barrier of her own selfhood. How can one give to the depth required in sexual, spiritual unity by denying the self? Is mutuality possible when either partner represses her or his feelings, whether they are joyous and seeking expression through physical union or discouraged and needful of tender understanding?

The "pursuit of cliched goals and values current in the present social milieu"[3] Sidney Jourard names as another barrier to autonomous action. To be eternally young and sexually attractive is a value of American culture pursued by both sexes. Susan Sontag illustrates the importance of a woman's body as a marketable product:

> From early childhood on, girls are trained to care in a pathologically exaggerated way about their appearance and are profoundly mutilated (to the extent of being unfit for first-class adulthood) by the extent of the stress put on presenting themselves as physically attractive objects. . . .[4]

Since personal worth for American females is tied to physical attractiveness, women spend countless hours trying to fill out or trim down their bodies to fit some norm of sexual appeal. "A woman's face is the canvas upon which she paints a revised, corrected portrait of herself."[5] The need to paint a corrected picture on one's face moves us farther and farther away from authenticity. Instead we maintain facades of usefulness, marketability, and worth as designated by the culture.

Akin to the priority Americans place on physical appearance is the importance we give to acquisitiveness and affluence. The woman who is not caught up in weekly or twice-weekly trips to the beauty parlor, frequent sorties to her favorite clothing boutique, regular visits with the Avon lady, the perennial home redecorating project, or the purchase of all kinds of consumer luxuries from perfume to parlor pillows is not considered a part of America's mainstream. Those who for economic reasons are unable to be a permanent part of the consumer elite, move in and out as they are financially able. Those totally outside often long to possess the respect, the power, the self-esteem that consumerism bestows on the consumers.

When a woman pursues clichéd goals rather than her own, she increasingly depends on others to do her thinking. Our "authorities" may include Ann, Amy, Abby, the president, the priest, the pastor, the polls. As one gives over her self-responsibility she eventually experiences a sense of powerlessness.

This sense of powerlessness, the fourth barrier to the development of autonomy, may cause one to live without hope or to misuse power. Powerlessness affects all human beings, though I will talk about its particular effects on women. With only a small stretch of the imagination the reader will think of dozens of ways men and children are caught in similar predicaments.

Women, particularly Christian women, grow up believing they should be self-sacrificing. Consequently, they are propelled into good works of all kinds and are expected to put the needs of others before their own. For this discussion it must be clear that I am not confusing mature sharing, mutually giving love (which are marks of an autonomous personality) with less healthy, almost manipulative acts done in the guise of Christian charity. Many of the teachings about self-sacrifice have had the effect of alienating a woman from herself. Frequently, the church has taught that giving thought to oneself is evil; thus, women deny themselves, try to lose themselves in others, and end up living with a high degree of intolerance and hostility. What has gone wrong?

When one is admonished to fulfill herself through someone else, she develops a dependency on that relationship. Her boundaries, her purpose are defined for her within the context of that relationship. Perhaps a brief examination of our child abuse problem in America will illustrate this point.

The ability to think, to act, to create is essential to the healthy human personality; any inhibition or abnegation of that need must produce tension and a temporary state of ill health. Biologically, women have the need to create potentially satisfied. But life does not, either for mother or child, culminate in pregnancy and birth. What happens to the woman whose entire, vibrant being has been given to procreation when the babe no longer needs to be suckled, when the growing child cries for independence? What becomes of the woman who, believing that through absorption in others, through being all-giving, all-loving, all-soothing, all-caring she will be fulfilled and blessed, finds that those to whom *she* needs to sacrifice herself are no longer dependent on her nurturant capacities or now seek, not her absorption in them, but instead someone with whom to struggle, to think, to laugh, to encourage their own freedom because she believes in and cherishes her own autonomy?

The conclusion is all too obvious. I assert that much of the impatience with childlikeness, the attempt to have children perform in adult-like ways, the desire to *push* our children into any experience—socializing at two, printing at three, reading at four, the unspoken, yes, usually denied, competition between parents for "successful" offspring—gives evidence to our confusion about self-sacrifice. What a horrendous pressure we place on physically small and psychologically young lives when we try to fulfill ourselves through them. If our feelings of worthlessness are unresolved in our acts of self-sacrifice, is it understandable that we resort to stronger means to control, to hang on to, and to secure our personal lives?

The kind of cruelty we have been talking about here is not the beating and bruising kind by which we are horrified and by which we excuse our occasional verbal tirades against the waywardness of our youngsters. What we have described is the subtle cruelty which, because I may not be in touch with myself as a productive, creative, autonomous human being, forces me to cripple my child's development toward freedom and love of self, the world, and others.

If we feel separated from ourselves as whole, autonomous human beings, how can we move toward autonomy and away from self-rejection and destruction of others? What is the path toward union and health for the Christian? Why hasn't the institutional Christian church led the way in revealing the nature of personhood? Has the institutional church seen only dimly what Jesus revealed about selfhood?

Our inner confusion about selfishness and selflessness arises from the ancient and current belief in human sinfulness and human separation discussed in Chapter 2. Interpretations of the biblical accounts of creation stress not the basic unitive purpose of God's creation but the separation (between people and God, man and woman, races and nations) assumptions prevalent in some of Judaism and Hellenism. Because the church has emphasized alienation and sinfulness in the stories of creation and because we have not fully comprehended the mission of Christ, we live burdened by our separations. Thus, all our perceptions about ourselves and about our human relationships are conditioned by the theme of alienation.

Even though we glibly acknowledge that Jesus taught wholeness, liberation, and reconciling relationship, we continue intellectually and psychologically to clutch tightly the beliefs of human sinfulness and alienation that underlie our society. We seek to atone for that sin and alienation by performing uncharacteristically Christlike acts of service that are motivated by self-denial rather than self-love and genuine concern for our sister or brother. Because of our commitment to our belief in basic sinfulness we condemn and reject those sisters and brothers who do not practice our particular form of "goodness." According to Jesus, it is only as we love our sisters and brothers whom we have seen that we can approach an understanding of loving God. "If someone says, 'I love God,' yet hates his brother, he is a liar. For he cannot love God, whom he has not seen, if he does not love his brother whom he has seen." (1 John 4:20, *Good News for Modern Man*) As a Christian church we must bear the burden for transmitting perverted beliefs about God and divine intention for humanity.[6]

What *did* Jesus teach about selfhood? Jesus, as the incarnation of God, revealed God's mission in creation: to make real the unity of humanity among human beings and with God. Through Jesus Christ God came to meet living, in-the-flesh beings. God became flesh and is flesh in and through us. "To be a human being means that we become symbolically one flesh with the other. . . ."[7] In order to accept God's presence in us and in turn our unity with all other beings of spirit and flesh, we cannot reject ourselves. The self for each of us, as for Christ, is the gift of God; it is the incarnation of God; it is the reentry of divinity into humanity upon each individual birth. What more sacred commentary can be made about selfhood?

Jesus' message was for all humanity but it was shared particularly with the oppressed who received it unskeptically. For them, labeled as the unclean of the society, left to beg in the streets and at the gates of the synagogues, Jesus offered wholeness not through their deeds or by their might or by their position but because they were of the unity of God. As Paul Tournier illustrates in *The Whole Person in a Broken World,* Jesus' instructions to the spirits of people were to know whose they were and to be reconciled to God. One cannot, I think, be at one with God and be unreconciled to oneself.

Jesus Christ, as the incarnation of God, offers the hope of newness and unity for each person. In understanding and accepting the incarnation of Christ and its relationship to our own incarnations, we become new creatures; we then comprehend the intent of Colossians 3:11 " . . . but Christ is all, and in all." If the incarnation of Christ was principally to teach us about our own nature and our relationship to God and all the rest of creation, we dare not, we simply cannot, remain in our old form and retain our former habits of thought and behavior.

That is to say, we can no longer believe in our own inferiority and ineptitude. We are new beings, not only to others, but to ourselves as well. We cannot resist the need and the desire to love ourselves, to believe in the person we are and are becoming. In loving ourselves in the present there is perpetual newness. Love awakens. It is hostility and hatred that cause the sleep of the self and rejection of God and the universe. Yet, for many of us, we have attempted to know God through hostility, believing that to love ourselves was showing contempt for God.

Contrary to making us arrogant or selfish, the recognition of God in us, the love of self as a cherished gift, makes movement toward others impossible to avoid. The autonomous, self-loving person seeks others, not to lean on them or to destroy them or to use them, but to know them as further revelation of God. Thus, "Christ is in all" takes on meaning for us and we progress more closely to comprehending,

> Do not lie to one another, seeing that you have put off the old nature with its practices and have put on the new nature, which is being renewed in knowledge after the image of its creator. Here there cannot be Greek and Jew, circumcised and uncircumcised, barbarians, Scythians, slave, free man, but Christ is all, and in all (Colossians 3:9-11).

Jesus' reactions to three women in the New Testament reveal yet more concretely his beliefs about personhood and particularly his attitude toward women as a part of the whole humanity.

In Luke 7:36-50 the story of Jesus' visit to the Pharisee's house is related. There he is greeted by a woman of ill-repute who bathes his feet in perfume and dries them with her hair. Simon and the other men in Jesus' company are disgusted not merely by the woman but by Jesus' tolerance of her action, and they speak contemptuously of her. Jesus does not reject her, though according to social custom then and now, he could have done so on several counts. Instead he offers a parable about forgiveness to those present, the message of which is: The person who is forgiven more will love more.

The woman must have had a belief in herself that transcended her awareness of her social unworthiness and made it possible for her to encounter Jesus. Jesus confirms her selfhood through his acceptance of her as one who has faced herself and is a forgiven, new creation. Jesus understands that she understands what selfhood and servanthood mean together and says to her, "Your faith has saved you; go in peace" (Luke 7:50).

Mary and Martha are characterized as close friends of Jesus. In the Luke 10:38-42 story of one of Jesus' visits to their home, Jesus forthrightly speaks for the greater importance of searching for truth, of hearing his teachings as opposed to caring for the physical details of livelihood. Jesus does not suggest that only men should hear or that only men are capable of comprehending his words. To a woman, Mary, he gives his personal welcome and blessing, in the company of men, for realizing what is the real food of life, for seeking through relationship with Jesus to know herself. To Martha, who is attending the household details, he says that she is too worried with unimportant matters. It may serve us all well, churchwomen and churchmen, to read frequently Jesus' evaluation of what is of significance in life.

In John 8, Jesus' attitude toward a sinful woman caught in adultery, in particular, and to women in general, stands in sharp contrast to the prevailing social attitudes about women. The crowd clamors to stone the adulteress. Jesus sends the spokesmen for vengeance away, saying "Let him who is without sin among you be the first to throw a stone at her" (John 8:7). The crowd departs silently, and with that statement, he grants wholeness to the woman by acknowledging her sinfulness and by believing in her capacity to understand his forgiveness and affirmation. "Neither do I condemn you; go, and do not sin again" (John 8:11).

These three examples represent a superficial cross section of women living in Jesus' society: close friends who hungered for his message and the women of ill-repute. All shared in common their oppressed status as women in a patriarchal society. Each withstood the condemnation and criticism of family or society. None, in these examples, denied herself. Each demonstrated belief in herself and commitment to what (to whom, in this case) she considered vital for her life. Each was transformed by her self-affirmation and through relationship with Jesus. To all equally Jesus spoke acceptance and affirmed their worth, a revolutionary act for a man of Hebrew lineage in that time. If Jesus' message reached and, indeed, included women in his time, what is that same message doing to church people today?

The paradox of selfhood and servanthood is not unlike the paradox of sinfulness and forgiveness. The more genuinely authentic and autonomous we become, the less grasping and fearful we are and the more we reach out to love and to hold others deeply in relationship. For the woman whose sins were many there was not self-criticism and rejection but intense understanding of forgiveness and acceptance of her whole self.

Knowing oneself authentically as a being of God is the experience of salvation/liberation. And that has far-reaching implications for men as well as women and for the relationship between the sexes. In the experience of authenticity the need to relate to others through games or to defend oneself through power that manipulates others vanishes. In accepting self-responsibility one loses the need to preserve oneself. Through autonomy one gives up the isolation and self-gratification of individualism.

For men this will mean a reorientation of their lives away from aggressive, competitive, externally motivated work and toward more relational, cooperative, inner-directed lives. For women it will require rejection of passiveness, the acceptance of their responsibility to think, to make judgments, and to be self-respecting so that growth in compassion for the extended human family is encouraged. For male and female together, authenticity and autonomy should produce an awareness that fullness of human sexuality can never be understood in terms of opposition; thus, females and males will acknowledge one another as complements, not opposites, that together know wholeness and extend it to others in the human family.

Into My Own

Around your family dinner table ask each family member to think of one quality about herself for which she is grateful. In turn each member will try to guess what that quality is; in the guessing process everyone is learning the many ways in which he is appreciated.

For a couple of weeks consider spending a few minutes of your meditation time learning to know and love yourself in quietness. Notice what differences that experience seems to make in your relationships with others. Does it affect your awareness of God's presence?

Consider gathering with a small group to discuss your understanding of servanthood and selfhood. The many passages in the New Testament on servanthood should be helpful. What does "Come, follow me" require of us?

Chapter 6

OWNING OPPRESSION

The oppressed must be their own example in the struggle for redemption.—Paulo Freire

When Jesus called his disciples from among the lowly in status, the powerless of the community, he required them to choose autonomy. They left their nets and neighbors to be obedient to a high call. The same call exists today. Our decision to be autonomous human beings committed to *mishpat* and *sedequah* will significantly alter a society committed to individualism. In this chapter we will examine the links between personal and social oppression and project the influence our decisions for autonomy may have on the church and society.

Since the resurgence of women's liberation in the 1960s, feminists and non-feminists have expressed a variety of ideas about the needs of women and the goals of the feminist movement. More than ten years after the publication of Betty Friedan's *The Feminine Mystique* and the subsequent formation of groups like the National Organization of Women, Women's Political Caucus, Women's Equity Action League, and Redstockings, three conditions exist today that challenge the movement and raise important questions about oppression. These conditions bear examination.

First, despite the aspirations of many feminists that the women's movement would be the great equalizer for women and the coalition of all other movements for liberation, neither women nor men have united in the women's cause to bring about radical social change. Second, from reports of women's consciousness groups around the country and from my own experience in such groups, the basic concerns of women are personal and nonpolitical. Third, because the women's liberation movement has been predominantly a gathering of educated middle-class women, many observers are uncertain about the meaning of the term "oppression." Women themselves of differing economic and racial groups find it difficult to reach agreement about their oppression. Amid charges against the society or the "system" from blacks, Hispanic-Americans, Puerto Ricans, and women, we hear the question repeated, "Who is oppressing whom?" And we grow more confused about the nature of oppression.

During the early 1960s women's cries of oppression seemed to be directed against men, men individually and males collectively. To be sure, many of those outbursts were justified; men have received preferential treatment in jobs; widespread inequities in pay between women and men have been common; some men abused women by treating them as objects to be bought or coddled but not taken seriously; many men expected wives to provide free maid service, even when those same wives also held jobs away from the home. Women in the early stages of the movement believed, because all women had to live and work with men, that barriers of class, race, and education would be overcome, and the women's movement would eventually liberate all classes and races of the oppressed.

However, women gradually discovered that such unity seemed illusive; the divisions created by education, race, economic class, and social caste were not easily removed. As a result, some women began to attack the "system." This system, women contended, perpetuates oppression through the kinds of education one does or does not receive; this same system locks women out of job or career opportunities; this system discriminates against women in legal matters; this system gives highest regard, measured through money, to the professional jobs and lowest priority to services, such as child care. Consequently, we have a class and caste system from which liberation, or even within which fluidity of movement, is impossible.

What women, who had hopes for a massive transformation of the system, failed to understand was that

> . . . any multiclass movement tends to be dominated by its most privileged, hence most conservative members. (Good jobs, money, free time, education, connections, and so on, help people gain power in political movements just as in larger society.) Equally important, a movement that defines itself as half the population fighting the other half can have no realistic plan for taking power. In short, I am suggesting that the feminist movement, as such, is simply unequipped to carry out an economic revolution. Only people in the lower economic brackets—women and men both—have either the incentive or the potential numbers to accomplish such a task.[1]

Because women found themselves locked into the system at differing places, because communication between different economic classes and social castes is a system taboo, and because the majority of women active in the women's movement had little personal incentive for or understanding of the need for social changes, unified commitment to the liberation of women, or the freeing of society from a dehumanizing system, became an abandoned hope.

The result of the lost dream is that for many women the movement has taken on personal rather than political meaning. From one another they seek support for living in their present conditions. Some have little vision of, or share few efforts toward creating, a more just social order. Instead they wish for and prepare to secure positions within the present political and economic structures. Such is the analysis of Ellen Willis, writing in an article, "Economic Realities and the Limits of Feminism." When Willis suggested to a Midwest women's group that " . . . Women's Liberation— defined as self-determination for *all* women—required a major overhaul of our economic system . . . "[2] the response from one candid woman was, "Frankly, if Women's Liberation means sacrificing what I have, I'm not interested."[3]

This chapter is based on the assumption that both the oppressors and the oppressed are oppressed people and that we realize liberation from that oppression only by owning (accepting internally) oppression as our corporate way of life. In the preceding chapters we have examined ways in which many American women experience oppression. Now I want to relate the oppression of women to other forms of oppression and to ponder ways to find release from oppressive patterns with which we all have lived so long that they seem to be our very lives. To consider throwing them off strikes us with dread.

In the early stages of writing this book, I received in the mail two tapes from a woman I did not then know. I will call her Evelyn. She offered her story of oppression. Though identification with Evelyn's circumstances may seem difficult initially, her story illustrates several kinds of oppression American women may experience. I include parts of it as a means through which we can feel the pain and struggle of a sister. The cultural assumption of female inferiority that underlies many of our personal and social practices of sexual inequality increases the likelihood that experiences similar to Evelyn's happen daily to women.

"I was born in one of the plains states in 1932 to a sixteen-year-old mother and a twenty-one-year-old father. Fourteen months later my sister was born. My parents separated when I was two, and I lived with my grandparents and two aunts and uncles. . . . When my mother remarried for the first time, we moved to California in late 1940. It was there at the age of eleven that my stepfather began sexually molesting me in very subtle ways. By this age I was quite aware of boys as boyfriends, and at twelve my stepfather became more daring in his exploration of my body. This caused great turmoil for me, and I finally told my mother to keep her husband in her own bed. My mother attempted to stab my stepfather, and there was a messy, messy scene when the police were called, I was questioned, and my father locked up . . . for twenty-four hours. My mother, my sister, and I went to my stepfather's sister's home. There, pretending to help me and my mother, my uncle (my stepfather's brother-in-law) took me alone into a room and asked me, "Did he do this? Did he do that?" All the while he was having his own feel of my body. . . .

"Mother divorced her second husband; six weeks later she eloped across the state line with another man. My second stepfather was a professional gambler and drank off and on. One week we'd have five thousand dollars spread out on the bed; the next week there wouldn't be enough for lunch money. . . . While staying with an aunt and uncle I spoke out of turn to my uncle because he was beating his dog. He took out his Marine leather belt and beat me until the blood ran. I refused to apologize, and only my aunt's persistent pleading caused him to stop. . . .

"At fifteen I had complete responsibility for myself. I was dating highway officers, mechanics, bus drivers, men who were eager to have my company. And I did need company.

"Two months later a boyfriend from my hometown in California came and told me that he wanted to marry me. Marriage was a way to stay away from home and to ease our mutual loneliness. Joe and I got a sales job traveling across country; when Joe realized I had selling ability that he didn't and we were near Chicago we quit. There we both took jobs for a couple months to save enough money to return to California. Back in California I went to work in a diner. When Joe couldn't find a job I took a second job as a dancehall hostess. On the two jobs I worked nine hours. It was during my marriage to Joe that I believed I had become pregnant; after five months the doctor took X-rays and said emphatically that I was not, nor had I ever been, pregnant. This was a very traumatic blow for me, and I fantasized that I had given birth to a daughter. My girl friends, with whom I was living now because Joe had enlisted in the Army, became worried when I would talk to my baby. They called an old boyfriend who came and talked to me. After he left I took all the drugs I could find and was discovered by my friends who called an ambulance. I spent three days in a medical ward of a general hospital and then was transferred to a psychiatric ward. My mother was called; my husband came and cried and said he was sorry, but he couldn't help. It was my second stepfather who was instrumental in getting me out of the hospital by saying, "Evelyn, you're not crazy; you just need some help." He did give me faith in myself. For two weeks following my hospitalization I lived with my mother and visited the psychiatrist. After that for the next two years, I lived from rooming house to rooming house.

"Adam became my steady boyfriend; he was a leader of a wild, hot-rod gang. Adam was Armenian. In January of 1950 I realized that I was pregnant and told Adam about it. He refused to marry me because of the shame it would bring his family. I contacted the Salvation Army and a social worker. I also contacted a lawyer since

I needed a divorce from Joe. Then I found out that he had already divorced me; servicemen can do that. And he had remarried. I went to live in the Booth Memorial Home from March until June. Adam never visited me. In the Home I received my first awareness of God. They talked about Jesus and his life, and I was hungry for God's love and understanding. Adam had instructed me to give the baby up for adoption and then when I returned to our town he would marry me. But in June I wrote him and said that I had decided to keep the baby and was returning to town where my mother and sister had rented a house. Both were now divorced. Adam was very angry about this, that somebody was messing up our plans, but then if I really meant it he would try to get time off work to come to see me. He came and one weekend we got a marriage license and were married. He left immediately to go on his seasonal fruit-loading job and was gone for six weeks. Our son was stillborn August 7, 1950. Adam wouldn't leave the hard-top races to take me to the hospital. Adam's sister advised him to divorce me now since there was no child involved. She said that he didn't need someone like me and referred to me with the crude word "slut." But Adam said that he had married for good so he would not get a divorce. We went to live on a ranch with his twenty-two-year-old brother, sixteen-year-old brother, twelve-year-old sister, and nine-year-old brother in an old farmhouse; his mother had died in an accident leaving nine children under the age of seventeen.

"For two years I worked in a packing house, cooked and washed for all of us. The second summer I went to fruit camp and worked for six weeks there. Adam would remind me about my stories of salvation and would tell me that now he was my god. I worked hard to be the good Armenian wife. I learned the dishes to cook; I learned how to greet the relatives in their language. The spring of 1952 I discovered I was pregnant, and in September our son was born. I was elated. Two years later, on New Year's day, a daughter was born. Adam was angry for three reasons and told the doctor, "I struck out." First, the baby had not arrived in time to be a tax deduction for the old year; second, she was the second baby of the New Year, not the first; third, and worst of all, she was a girl. The doctor was furious and let Adam know that that kind of kidding was inappropriate. When our daughter was six months old I began to have anxiety feelings and asked the doctor for help. He referred me to the mental health agency. My mother had now remarried and lived about three miles from my home. I turned to her for help, but even after so many years she still could not help. During the counseling with the psychologist I found that I was pregnant a third time. Adam was still very indifferent to my needs as a person; the psychiatrist at that time asked me to consider a divorce, but I couldn't even discuss it. It was just unthinkable at that time. . . ."

Having given herself devotedly to her master husbands, Evelyn was at this point in her life largely an object, loveless and powerless, created and controlled by a social environment in which male supremacy is assumed.

One reason the women's liberation movement has been threatening to large numbers of people is that we are more comfortable thinking about oppression as something beyond our experiences and not touching our friends. When we hear the word oppression, we think perhaps of repressive governments, or economic and political varieties of oppression affecting American Indians, blacks, Hispanic-Americans, minorities within the culture. We hold this partial view of oppression innocently, though not justifiably: first, because we feel fairly closely tied to the social mainstream; and second, because to expand our understanding to include psychological oppression of women or the psychological effects of economic and political oppression threatens us personally. Instead of hearing the cries of women who feel oppressed, we dismiss the women as neurotic malcontents.

When we read stories like Evelyn's we are apt to feel sorry and then to dismiss them as isolated examples of injustice. In the following ways Evelyn's home environment plus the cultural attitudes about womanhood limited and confused her life. Just at the age when Evelyn was becoming aware of herself as a blossoming young woman, she was used pathologically as a sex object by an adult male. From another adult male she learned she should not speak against an authority, even in the presence of violence performed against an animal. Evelyn's loneliness and insecurity led her to an early marriage in hopes of filling her personal emptiness. Perhaps it was in part a need to experience a sense of worthiness or creativity unfulfilled in her marriage that caused Evelyn to fantasize a pregnancy and birth.

When Evelyn married Adam, she adopted his ways; she learned to speak his language and to prepare the native dishes. She cooked and washed for her husband's brothers and sisters, as well as worked in a packing house. Accord-

-ing to the culture it is a wife's duty to do the "woman's work" at home even though she, too, works outside the home. Adam told Evelyn that he was her god, but Evelyn's culture had conditioned her to accept that fact much earlier in her life.

In Evelyn's self-disclosure do we find traces of our own choices or experiences? How did we learn that it was desirable to be sexually attractive? For whom do we still strive to be pleasurable? Why and when did we marry? How earnestly have we worked to clean and cook up to "his" standard? Have we retained independence and equality in marriage? In what ways have we encouraged the nurturant qualities in others, particularly men, to develop? What isolation or ridicule have those who chose not to marry experienced? All of these questions should put us face to face with implicit and explicit social instruction for being female.

The extent to which such instruction is oppressive, because it defines rigidly what a female should be and do, can be determined only by each of us alone. If we leave Evelyn's story at this point, we possibly would conclude that she should not have married or should have married more cautiously. However, Evelyn's story is not an isolated experience; it invites us to probe the roots and the methods of oppression as well as some of the psychological phenomena involved in a widespread need to oppress or to be oppressed.

Frantz Fanon, black psychoanalyst, author of the influential analysis of oppression, *The Wretched of the Earth,* has demonstrated, in his studies of colonialism and racism, that any prevailing form of oppression is inextricably linked to the cultural system of which it is a part and is determined by the historical circumstances that created the particular culture. To oppress is not the deliberate intent of malicious individuals but rather a result of a complex culture and history. Thus, we cannot study individual instances of oppression without simultaneously questioning our culture, and specifically its economic, political, and religious systems and beliefs that have created and sustained unjust relationships, inside and outside America.[4]

Oppression is essentially a distorted power relationship. Those who hold power see it as a necessary condition of social, political, or economic control and organization. Those dominated by the powerful know it as a corrupting means of coercing people. Erich Fromm and Rollo May suggest, however, that the drive toward power within the human being is as natural and essential as the desire to love and to be loved; therefore, it is not power in itself which we need to accept or to reject but the uses of it that we need to understand and incorporate healthfully into our lives.

Derived from the Latin *posse,* power means *to be able.* Power is the capacity of being able: able to act, to think, and to create. Power in American society is understood as a force to be grasped or as a status to be achieved by a few to control many. Even when we talk of power interpersonally, we speak of it not as an enabler for individual expression but as a device of domination. In the traditional American marriage relationship, power is usually expressed in its oppressive form as a means used commonly by the male, the dominant leader, to direct the lives of his family. If it is true, as Fromm and May suggest, that power is a psycho-physical drive of *all* human beings, what has altered our understanding of power from a sense of *being able* to one of control and manipulation?

To have a concept of *being able* when one holds a concept of the world as divided between subjects and objects, good deeds and bad deeds, dark and light, permanent separations *ad infinitum,* forces one to conceptualize being able only "over against" someone or something else. Hence, power is viewed not as an integrating drive within one's own life and between lives, but as a means by which one relates outwardly to control objects (animate or inanimate) or by which one's own life is directed and manipulated from without. Because oppression is tenaciously rooted in power that dominates and controls, we must ask whether oppression could exist if our understanding of the nature of the world were not dichotomic, "over against," and if we knew power as a personal enabling force, as a means of unification rather than domination and division? I think it could not.

Relationships in which power is wielded by a superior over an inferior threaten to be oppressive. When such relationships are temporary and fluid, allowing all parties at some time to exchange places or to move on to other relationships, oppression of any intensity is probably not suffered. It is the inequitable relationship that endures by cultural rites and social organization and is of economic, political, or psychological necessity that turns into oppression. The long-term, dehumanizing effects of unequal power relationships, controlled by social myth and custom, deny full humanity to an individual or a group by several means.

Conquest

Colonialism results from the conquest by a dominant nation of a smaller or weaker group of people. Colonial conquest involves more than mere territorial gain; colonialists, separated from their personal sense of being able, seek to demonstrate their worth by mastering the soil, the seats of government, the schools, and the marketplace of their so-called inferiors. And most insidiously, often historically in the guise of altruism, humanism, enlightenment, or Christian virtue, the colonialists ravish the bodies, souls, and minds of the natives by denying the birth ways of the natives, the traditions of their culture, their native languages, and their religions. Conquest is always an "over against" power relationship from which the vanquished can never be extricated. The conquered, severed from their cultural roots, lose their authentic identities in attempting to be assimilated into the colonizing culture. Likewise, the colonialists are never free when they engage in conquest because they cannot relate openly and share mutually with those they dominate.

Isolation

Isolation is a means of repressing persons who, if permitted to be together, could challenge the authority of the controller or who by their personal example might inspire revolution in the minds of others. Examples abound from our current experience and from the history of isolated groups of people; ghettoes, reservations, and American suburban homes harbor those whose presence is a real or imaginary threat to the powerful.

American women could not be put on reservations alone, but the nuclear family functions perhaps even more detrimentally to isolate females from the center of social, economic, and political life, separated from one another and from nearly all natural adult intellectual and emotional exchanges. The private home, as a social phenomenon, may operate as an instrument of isolation.

Elizabeth Janeway criticizes our current concept of home as a nuclear family unit dominated principally by a mother who, with her children, is isolated from the outside world. Our present concept, which many people believe to be a divinely designed and ordained institution, is a relatively recent invention of the middle class. The Old English *ham* or Gothic *heim* was used to describe a primitive sense of village. By the fourteenth century "home" meant native village or birthplace, and by the sixteenth century the definition was altered slightly to mean "one's own place or country." Before 1700, when the first notion of home as a small secure unit set off from the noise of the world appeared, the women of the villages were workers in the fields or managers of farms and workshops.[5]

The American wife, who makes homemaking and child-rearing her major functions, lives many of her days surrounded by walls and furniture, restricted to the tremendous psychological and physical demands of children. Her own emotional and intellectual needs as an independent subject may go unmet. She often does not have a community or village to sustain her and to which she can offer her special skills and insights.

Women who are unattached to men are perhaps even more disastrously relegated to loneliness. They may try to escape that loneliness by seeking relief from other females in similar situations or through their attachment to a job or an important boss. The aged of both sexes experience the feelings of worthlessness arising from the isolation that comes when they are sent (or even when they choose to go) to "old folks' homes" or retirement centers. There they stay to live out their remaining contributionless days, unrelated to a heterogeneous world of vitality.

Manipulation

Two areas of present American life that are highly manipulative of women are the capitalistic economic system and the Judeo-Christian religious tradition. In a capitalistic economy, competition rooted in individualism rather than cooperation is encouraged as the mode of working and as the basis for measuring personal success. Money is the gain sought for work done; money in turn buys symbols of success—the automobiles and boats, the home, and the kinds of leisure that assure one of personal worth. Those who can work and make money are guaranteed a certain kind of potency in the American society. Those who do not have money and the status accompanying it are valued less and are controlled by the economically powerful.

Generally, white males are the major wage earners in the American economy; and blacks, male and female, and white women float in and out of that economy as their personal or family needs demand or as the society dictates. They usually receive less pay for equal jobs. Marketplace manipulation directs women and men season by season to want what is the appropriate or important produce for the competitive, successful person. Advertisers promise personal worth for purchasing competitively those items that are in vogue and for rejecting those that have lost prestige. "The look is you," or "For the woman who knows. . . ," or "Make others notice you. . . ," we are told.

A woman's lust for possessions has been learned from an acquisitive, materialistic society and from questionable religious ideas about the nature of woman. Within Christianity, historically women have been manipulated to believe that they are submissive, subservient to men; they have been told that biological motherhood and a life of self-denial are a female's crowning glories and have therefore chosen to live their lives for and through others.

At an earlier time when women may have chosen to live lives of Christlike service, they renounced worldly competition. Now with pronouncements about the death of God and the difficulty of distinguishing between the church and the Kiwanis Club, women are left with feelings of uncertainty and emptiness about their own lives and purposes. Because they may not have grown up to the stature of Christ, they are tempted to fill their emptiness with things dictated by advertisers and manufacturers.

Exploitation

Both exploitation and manipulation are means by which people are used skillfully for someone else's advantage. The best example of female exploitation is the well-known use of women in the labor force in the cause of national defense during wartime. In the Civil War women kept the farms and businesses going often single-handedly; they nursed the injured, did relief work, and in the North argued the issue of slavery.

An important way to mobilize people, particularly in time of national crisis, is to appeal to their patriotism. Out of strong feelings of national responsibility, in a country where they were not yet granted a vote, women joined the labor force during World War I in blast furnaces and armaments factories. They worked around high explosives and manufactured agricultural implements. Those who tried to keep alive the issue of women's suffrage at the same time they supported the country in industry were charged angrily with anti-patriotism.[6]

When the war was over many women's jobs disappeared, and other women were laid off from the work they had undertaken. Propaganda about the place of woman at home began to reappear. What individual women wanted or needed for their own development was of little consideration; they were a commodity now out of date in a postwar economy. A husband, speaking in Thomas Cottle's article "A Middle American Marriage," makes the following observation about women in the working force of America:

> When women work it's a fill-in. They substitute, and brother, when they put in the substitute it's because the first team either stinks or can't play. Or maybe . . . 'cause the first team's got a lead they'll never catch . . .[7]

In an economic and political system that (1) equates personal worth with the ability to make money, (2) bestows increasing prestige on those who have the greatest sums of money, and (3) uses women workers as substitutes, is there any condition except exploitation and ultimate oppression for the American female?

Conquest, isolation, manipulation, and exploitation are all means by which a superior in an inequitable power relationship may control an inferior; and all these means have been used or supported by virtually all our social institutions, including the Christian church. These means encourage a system that is oppressive to humanity.

From what internal labyrinths does the need to oppress fellow human beings arise? What are our own motives to control or to be controlled? Why have we so easily accepted oppressive social, political, and religious systems?

Both the need to oppress and the tolerance of oppressive conditions grow out of fear and a flight from freedom. The process of individuation through which every human organism moves outward into the world produces two results in us: (1) we experience the self in all its individuality and strength, and (2) we become aware of aloneness as we never have before. The feeling of aloneness causes anxiety in us, and we perhaps try to flee from freedom to the submissive state we knew as pre-individualized selves. In the return to submission and dependence we ultimately find greater insecurity that festers into hostility and resentment against ourselves and those to whom we cling.

A likely result of the hostility born of rejected freedom is a need to strike out against those to whom one has given oneself as their object. Thus, we begin to understand the kinship of oppressed and oppressor. And we begin to expect to find that those who oppress have themselves been dominated in the past. As we reject independence because of our fear of freedom, we are moved only deeper into fear and powerlessness.

Karen Horney goes to the roots of Jewish culture to explain the causes of contemporary oppression of the female by a malist society. Referring to two incidents from the story of Adam and Eve, she explains the fear of woman in the following way:

> First of all, woman's capacity to give birth is partly denied and partly devaluated: Eve was made of Adam's rib and a curse was put on her to bear children in sorrow. In the second place, by interpreting her tempting Adam to eat of the tree of knowledge as a sexual temptation, woman appears as the sexual temptress, who plunges man into misery. I believe that these two elements, one born out of resentment, the other out of anxiety, have damaged the relationship between the sexes from the earliest times to the present.[8]

Karen Horney has further suggested that "it is contrary to human nature to sustain appreciation without resentment toward capabilities one does not possess."[9] In a dualistic culture which emphasizes individualism and separation, rather than wholeness and ultimate union of all creation, Horney's supposition seems logical. Therefore, accepting her conclusion that one cannot appreciate over a long period of time capabilities different from her or his own, one has to do something with the antagonism felt against the person who is different. Such antagonism is organized, for example, into strong social myths about the nature of woman; and individual women are dealt with oppressively through culturally accepted *rites of oppression.*

One rite of oppression is to objectify the fear or dread one feels. Men attempt to deal, Horney reports, with their dread of the female by rationalizing,

> "It is not," he says, "that I dread her; it is that she herself is malignant, capable of any crime, a beast of prey, a vampire, a witch, insatiable in her desires. She is the very personification of what is sinister."[10]

A second rite of oppression is to keep in subjugation that which one resents and fears. Many patriarchal cultures past and present have such rites.

> . . . the Miri in Bengal do not permit their women to eat the flesh of the tiger, lest they become too strong. The Watawela of East Africa keep the art of making fire a secret from their women, lest women become their rulers. The Indians of California have ceremonies to keep their women in submission; a man is disguised as a devil to intimidate the women. The Arabs of Mecca exclude women from religious festivities to prevent familiarity between women and their overlords. We find similar customs during the Middle Ages—the Cult of the Virgin side by side with the burning of witches; the adoration of "pure" motherliness, completely divested of sexuality, next to the cruel destruction of the seductive woman.[11]

The historic and current concept of God as the male, the father, in a male-oriented culture, inescapably an authority figure, serves in many cases to keep women in subjugation to males. A woman's earthly relationship to men has frequently been an unequal one. To the extent that one's spiritual relationships tend to mirror earthly ones, a woman's relationship with God is often an authoritarian one. In such a relationship she further internalizes attitudes of subjugation.

The rites of oppression of women that institutions overly practice around the country grow from these psycho-sacred beliefs and habits of the culture. Paying women less for equal work; divesting them of rank, position, and decision-making functions; refusing recognition of outstanding accomplishments; ignoring the essential nurturing functions traditionally performed by women—all these are rites arising from fear of another human being, from the need to keep that human being within one's control.

I have a friend on the faculty of a church-related institution of higher education who has been associated with that institution for thirty years. She created, and singly staffed, the department of accounting, when it was demanded; yet, when a man joined the department to help teach the growing number of students interested in the field, she was required, not asked, to give the upper-level courses which she had designed and taught for five years to the incoming man. Twenty years after this incident, when a public relations brochure was issued about the department, her name was omitted as the initiator of the department. Her salary and fringe benefits were always less than the salaries and benefits for her male counterparts until the Civil Rights Amendment required by law that there be no discrimination in employment opportunities on the basis of race, color, religion, sex, or national origin. In this case, the state outpaced the Christian church in doing justice and rejecting certain rites of oppression that exploit women.

Both women and men fear freedom but cope with that fear in basically different ways. Women may attempt to return to the security of submission. Because such return is ultimately impossible, women who try this usually experience hostility. That hostility they turn inward against themselves. Men, on the other hand, deal with their fear of freedom by objectifying it, projecting it onto others, and then trying to subjugate the objects of their fear. The female professor just described began to understand her frustrations only two years ago. Prior to that time she thought the discriminatory treatment of her was a product of her imagination or an outgrowth of her selfish desire for fairness or recognition.

The social and religious lessons which teach women to be long-suffering and eternally kind may conspire to keep a woman from being an authentic self that must say, "I am" boldly. The most tragic result of learning such lessons too well is that many women deeply repress especially their negative feelings and believe themselves to be never angry or hurt.

Treating persons as objects, as a means of dealing with our own rejected freedom, may mean that we no longer have to take a particular person or group seriously. But it does cut us off from vital human exchange. Bereft of such dynamic interchange, we turn to other objects and personalize them. Inanimate objects that have no living thought or emotion seem safe to receive our emotional attachments.

Cars and boats often bear terms or names of endearment. Anne Sexton's "Housewife" gives words to this phenomenon for a female.

> Some women marry houses.
> It's another kind of skin; it has a heart,
> a mouth, a liver and bowel movements.
> The walls are permanent and pink.
> See how she sits on her knees all day,
> faithfully washing herself down.
> Men enter by force, drawn back like Jonah
> into their fleshy mothers.
> A woman *is* her mother.
> That's the main thing.[12]

By either method—objectifying human beings or personifying lifeless objects—you are insulated from dialogue with yourself and others.

I submit that our tendency to objectify people out of our own fears is a societal phenomenon and a partial explanation as to why we fail in the United States to meet human needs but can continue to meet ever-soaring materialistic and militaristic needs. If we were socially committed to meeting human needs, would situations like the following persist and increase?

When a woman is head of a household she has less earning power than single white male parents. With her smaller earning power she often is without adequate child care or savings. The only alternative for such a woman may be public welfare which in 1970 paid an average of $49.65 a month per recipient through Aid to Dependent Children. In 1974 the amount of aid to families with dependent children was roughly $218 per family per month. To house, feed, and clothe a family on that amount is difficult. In describing her experiences as a welfare mother Marie Ratagick reports that the supplemental welfare program is the most misunderstood benefit.

> . . . a woman worked four hours a night cleaning offices for $1.65 an hour, but when she reported it honestly, the [welfare] worker said, "Well, now that you've got a job, I guess you'll be getting off welfare, won't you?" Because the woman didn't know her right to supplemen-

tal welfare, she didn't protest—and later on, the worker said, "You told me to take you off welfare." That's what makes women lie about the pittance they earn, and then be subject to fines and even jail sentences as "welfare cheaters."[13]

Because many insurance companies still operate with the belief that the man is the protector, women may have no insurance policies on their own lives or their benefits may be significantly less than their male counterpart. Pennsylvania's Insurance Commissioner, Herbert S. Denenberg, investigated such discrimination in the insurance industry. In a preliminary study Denenberg and a task force of Pennsylvania women found the following:

> In health insurance . . . maternity benefits may be far below the average costs of pregnancy and childbirth. Female employees in group insurance plans may receive smaller maternity benefits than the wives of male employees. The pregnancy expenses of dependent female children often are not covered at all. . . . Women frequently are unable to buy disability policies that provide income for more than three years, while men can buy policies that will pay from the time of disability until the man is 65. . . ."[14]

The late 1976 decision by the United States Supreme Court to grant individual corporations the right to offer or to withhold maternity benefits for women further strengthens the power corporations have over individual lives and makes clear our social commitment to put business interests before the service of human needs.

Obtaining credit for married women, even when they are supporting husbands, is difficult. When women are divorced, separated, or widowed it may be impossible to secure credit. In some instances women seeking loans have had to sign affidavits that they would not have children during a specified period of time.

The tax system assumes that only two-income families will have deductible expenses such as child care. A married woman who is self-employed, without income for a period of time but in need of child care in order to carry on her work, cannot deduct those expenses from the joint return she and her husband file. Men whose wives are at home to care for children may not take any deductions for that care; the implication that a woman's work in the home is not worthy of remuneration is clear. In two-income families the second income usually puts the family into a higher tax bracket, thus discouraging the second job, which is often the woman's.

An assistant professor of economics at Princeton University, Harvey S. Rosen, shows additional ways in which tax laws discriminate against married working women. From his research one understands how tax laws may be rooted in the assumption that when a woman marries she should be cared for by her husband's income in return for services rendered to him. By penalizing couples both of whom wish to remain economic contributors, the tax system, in effect, supports a feudalistic notion of marriage. While the law does give married couples the option of filing separate income tax statements, these "separate" forms are treated differently than the forms filed by unmarried people. In an article about Rosen's research appearing in the February 21, 1977 *Princeton Weekly Bulletin,* Rosen indicates that the taxes paid by two unmarried people with incomes of $18,000 would jump $1,320 if they married and filed jointly.

In some areas of the country lawnmowing rates for high school youth have jumped from $1.00 or $2.00 an hour three years ago to $10.00 for a lawn that takes an hour to mow. Child care rates have barely increased in the same amount of time. In fact, when I babysat as a high school student eighteen years ago, I earned $.50 an hour. Today competent high school babysitters receive $1.00 an hour; qualified mothers who provide child care for other children receive perhaps $2.00 an hour. Such practices perpetuate the cultural notion that men (who usually have lawn jobs) earn more than women (who usually have the child care positions). More importantly, these figures tell us unequivocally something about our real values.

It should not be surprising, when one follows such examples of discrimination against human needs to their logical conclusions, to find that the United States government in 1973 spent $78 billion on military expenditures compared to $36 billion on health services and care. (See

Ruth Sivard's *World Military and Social Expenditures,*
1976) Nor should we be puzzled to learn that a group like
the Trilateral Commission, from whom President Carter
selected many of his advisors, has suggested that in developing an international economic system the rich, developed
nations of Europe, Japan, and the United States should
decide among themselves about the changes necessary to
assist the economic development of the Third World rather
than to give the Third World countries broad political participation in such decisions. Oppression experienced individually is always related to a larger social fabric of values
and vested interests that require our fearless examination.

Assuming that we are able to face some of the oppressive conditions in the society that affect women in particular, how can we break the cycle of oppression? A major
obstacle to breaking the cycle is the tendency of those who
have been treated as objects and have thereby been oppressed to seek to become like those who hold power.
Women, denied full humanity, may seek to become like men
in order to receive what has always been their right to
have—wholeness and respect as persons. In our culture, we
naively assume that the way out of oppression is simply to
move into power politically and economically. And the kind
of power that we know best by example is power that
manipulates and dominates, not participatory power that is
shared with all.

Paulo Freire believes that the first step in overcoming
oppression is to make the feelings of oppression more painful by looking at them carefully and owning oppression as
one's own state of being. When we are able to feel our hurts
and anger, we are much more likely to feel others' pain and
then to break the isolation that oppressions tend to generate
by joining with other oppressed people.

To own oppression we must take off our false faces, especially for ourselves. We must put aside our compulsion to
believe what we have been told about ourselves or about
what roles we are to play when such advice runs against our
genuine experiences. We must admit anger and frustration.

We must believe in our own worth at the same time that we own oppression. We must believe that oppression is not a humane way to live; it is a perversion of God's intent for humanity.

Evelyn, in the first illustration of this chapter, believed the instructions that the social milieu in which she had grown up had given about women: they are patient, unassuming, passive, and devoted to men. After twenty-five years she also had internalized her stepfather's and her husbands' attitudes about her worthlessness. Did she ever feel hostility, anger, resentment toward them? Yes, but for the most part that hostility was turned inward. Each passing year she repudiated Adam's unfair vituperations less, because to do so was unfeminine, unchristian and uncharacteristic of a "good" wife.

Instead of repressing felt anger, hurt, or hatred, Freire says we must accept those feelings, dwell on them enough to know that they belong to us and why we have them. Evelyn eventually was able to do this and through that act owned her oppression.

After the birth of her third child, she began to take a different look at herself. She attended a church in the community where she had been treated with compassion and respect. At this time she nursed Adam's brother during his terminal illness. For the last three weeks of his life Evelyn was beside Sam's bed twenty-four hours a day. His faith sustained her, and she recalls praying aloud by his coffin, "God, if there is a God, show yourself to me."

The following month Evelyn joined the church she had been attending. "I learned to know Christ personally," she said, "and experienced forgiveness and joy overflowing." She decided to finish high school by going to night classes. When her two sons showed brainwave irregularity on an EEG test and she was advised to obtain help at a child guidance center, Adam became furious. He told Evelyn she was crazy, not his sons, and he refused to counsel with the doctors. Her sons were denied treatment as a result. In her anguish she turned to a Christian counselor who had her read *Guilt and*

Grace by Tournier; she continued prayerfully to seek direction for her life.

By 1965 Evelyn was interested in nurses training. She applied to a school and was accepted. She babysat for four other children before and after classes to pay her tuition. After two months of classes Adam said she must quit because going to school was breaking up their marriage. She quit and tried to counsel with Adam.

When it seemed that reconciliation was impossible, Evelyn decided to get a divorce. That decision left her alone. Adam threatened to go to her church and tell everyone there what a deserter she was and how God had twisted her head. Some few people in the church asked her to resign from her position as children's director in view of her circumstances. Her parents asked her not to come to their home if she left her husband, and Adam's family succeeded in keeping the children from her even when she was to have all of them together.

Evelyn sought the best job she could get to support herself and her daughter, of whom she had custody. She finally got a job as a nurse's aide. A year and a half after her divorce she married a widower. After many ugly scenes between Adam, the children, and Evelyn, with her new husband and her daughter she moved to the East. There Evelyn finished nursing school. "I am knowing now for the first time in my life what it is like to love and be loved as an equal, as a person of worth," she said.

Owning our oppression, however great or small, links us with other isolated, oppressed people. By giving up isolation, which is a technique of oppression, we begin to break the circle of oppression. Black Americans have shown us what joint effort can do; communion makes blackness beautiful where before, in isolation, blackness was sinister. Groups of women are now doing the same thing—supporting one another and affirming their inherent worth. Females who get in touch with their authenticity make womanhood powerful in the creative sense.

One of the most urgent functions of breaking out of the

isolation of oppression is to raise questions about oppression with other people. We must ask: Who are the oppressed? Who or what are my oppressors? What is the nature of a system that measures human worth in power terms? Why do I covet my oppressor's position and power? How do I feel about my oppression? What views do I hold toward others who are oppressed and toward my oppressors? What are my lost ambitions and dreams? What do I envy in my oppressor? What do I covet for myself? What do I hope for the world? What do I feel in the presence of my oppressor? From where do I receive strength for living?

The anticipated outcome of this kind of searching analysis is the growing ability to accept one's own behavior and ideas as valid. Owning, as opposed to denying, one's personal oppression is the first step toward liberation because it demands total commitment to the worth of selfhood specifically and universally.

When we own oppression personally and communally, we have the potential to "restore the humanity"[15] of both the oppressed and the oppressor. In concrete terms, how can this restoration occur?

First, of course, one must believe that the oppressor because of her or his fear is oppressed herself or himself. Such a connection arises from the knowledge that dehumanization occurs wherever a person denies the life of another or when one's own life is controlled by someone else. When a person acknowledges the oppression of the oppressor, she or he is forced to view the oppressor as a sister or a brother, not as an evil opponent. Oppressor and oppressed are brought together in a radical union from which liberation can be born. It is impossible for

> the pursuit of full humanity . . . [to be] carried out in isolation or individualism, but only in fellowship and solidarity; therefore it cannot unfold in the antagonistic relations between oppressors and oppressed. No one can be authentically human while he prevents others from being so.[16]

The kind of union I am describing here must be understood as radical;[17] it is not, in any way, a continuation of the old order of superior and inferior. It requires that we (1) understand the hazards of assimilating the oppressor image within our own consciousness, and (2) interrupt the pattern of imitation. This assimilation of the oppressor image within oneself is one reason, I think, numerous women around the country so vociferously opposed the Equal Rights Amendment. The identity of these women opposing ratification is tied up with their male oppressors. Many do not know themselves apart from relationship with men.

These women offer adoration to the oppressor because they wish, if not to be in the position of men, to retain whatever "special privileges" they believe themselves to have been granted by men. They fear that, given equality, women will lose their position, their place of assumed respect with men. Most of these women do not know themselves to be oppressed, and even if some feel injustice or oppression in certain aspects of their lives, they have not fully owned oppression as theirs. Similarly, without a decision to interrupt our tendencies to imitate those in power, we are likely to pursue their paths to overcome oppression. Only by accepting our own unique humanity and refusing oppressive behavior will we move toward liberation.

From where do we get our models of liberation if we refuse to accept oppressor models of behavior? Difficult though it is to extricate oneself from a long history of oppressive prescriptions and social conditioning assigned to females, I think one's freedom is ultimately found, not in models, but within oneself. The highest human effort is *to be,* not *to be like.* There are too few models for such behavior.

In a social climate of conformity, imitation, and superficiality, genuine being is revolutionary behavior. As you gradually achieve a sense of your own being and are able to act out of your new knowledge, you humanely encourage others *to be.* The individual who chooses the radical direction of *being* oneself is involved in a revolutionary process. True revolutionaries love themselves, others, and the world because they live in a constant contact with their inner beings. The awakened inner being sees commonalities among people rather than differences and barriers.

Therefore, it is impossible for one in touch with such inwardness to participate in sustaining inequality, hierarchies, competitive and totalitarian relationships. A revolutionary, like Jesus, practices equality, is a sister or brother of other oppressed people throughout the world—the poor, the blacks, the American Indians, the colonized of every country—and views one's own cause as part of their causes. The revolutionary possesses within him or her a new world view that may yield new sensitivities and yet unknown coalitions of people to work unitedly for liberation.

When many *new beings* come together to name their oppression and to renounce their passive, permissive participation in that oppression, the old orders simply cannot stand; and slowly, ever so slowly, the trapped, oppressor and oppressed, are set free. "As the oppressed, fighting to be human take away the oppressors' power to dominate and suppress, they restore to the oppressors the humanity they had lost in the exercise of oppression."[18]

Into My Own

Within your family or/and among some friends, talk about ways in which you have oppressed others. Feel the feelings that thinking about that brings forth. Then talk about the ways in which you felt oppressed. Give everyone a turn to do both parts of such an exercise.

Use the questions on page 118 to discover more about yourself.

Chapter 7.

CULTIVATING A
RENAMED GARDEN

*To seek the liberation of women without losing [a] sense of
communal personhood is the great challenge and secret power
of the women's revolution. Its only proper end must be the
total abolition of the social pattern of domination and subjugation and the erection of a new communal social ethic.* —
Rosemary Reuther

Human beings in the women's movement, as part of all
liberation movements, are called to reveal a new humanity
that does not imitate the relationships and social structures
of the fallen creation. Such a radical revelation cannot come
without a spiritual rebirth both within and without the
church. Women and men will experience a spiritual renewal
to the extent that they understand the unitive nature of life.
In the lives of the Old Testament prophets and especially in
Jesus' life we will find examples of those who knew oneness
with God and solidarity with humanity. From that
wholeness Jesus offered himself as a servant of liberation.

Despite its historic institutional oppressiveness, the
church, as it discerns and follows the revolutionary teachings
of Jesus, will experience a spiritual awakening and may
become a gathering of new people who, with changed commitments, shape a new world. Our responsibility in looking
toward a renamed garden is: (1) to imagine what needs to
happen for women and men to know personal wholeness

and sexual mutuality; (2) to perceive the witness of the church in a renamed garden; and (3) to consider ways to cultivate a garden renamed for wholeness and reunion.

Liberation from oppressive fragmentation into wholeness occurs through admission—confession of one's oppressed state of existence. Even though our private lives may seem to carry fewer visible signs of oppression than do the lives of our sisters and brothers in Bangladesh, for example, we must hear what anyone who feels oppression is saying. For women this means an unflinching acknowledgment that the society, indeed the Western world, is dominated by males who uphold individualism, competition, and aggressiveness as virtues and who historically have degraded qualities linked with females.

As women we must accept that we have generally been passive or submissive to males or male-dominated institutions. We must study our personal and cultural life-scripts to see why we are living unsatisfying lives, if we are. We must not apologize for our nurturant or relational capacities, but we may need to confess that we have believed those valuable human qualities to be exclusively ours, that we have confined our lives to nurturant functions, or more recently that we have ourselves rejected nurturing and serving others in favor of individualistic goals that we hope will bring recognition in a male-oriented society. We must admit, where truthful, our dependence on intuition and our resistance to lucid and critical thinking.

We must accept responsibility for perpetuating a fallen creation by our lack of vision and mistrust in our imagination. We must acknowledge that as sexual beings we have exploited men and have permitted the exploitation of ourselves by them, rather than cherished one another, because we have separated our bodies from our spirits and have tried to spiritualize our physical beings. In owning the oppressed condition of our half-lives we may find latent talent and strength; simultaneously we may experience the desire to know other half-persons.

The courage required to own oppression carries with it

an implicit faith that oppression is not the natural, or divinely intended, order of creation. This underlying faith urges us to know ourselves as beings of God and of an orderly universe. As we learn that, we will think anew about political, economic, religious issues of our time rather than to feel victimized. We will act on our best judgments about educating children, for example, or lobbying for human rights. We may learn new skills, such as motor mechanics or finances, that we have believed we would never need to develop.

Out of acceptance of our corporate oppression we will extend our compassion and nurture perhaps by establishing neighborhood cooperative child care, by developing parent education programs, or by encouraging global perspectives and peace education in our schools. We might do more to create centers to which people could go for reflection or counsel in moments of despair. In moving toward liberation we will refuse to give ourselves over to "authorities" who will tell us what to be or do. We will resist the impulse to play "Squash" and will encourage men to talk about themselves or to take a year off from a job to learn to know their children or to have time for personal growth.

We will make contact with nature that includes a love for our physical bodies. In the relationship with our mates we will initiate lovemaking and pursue our beloved. As we join such newly discovered qualities with our already developed ones, we may know for the first time what it means to have power in the inner sense of *being able*. With such an experience of power one can no longer be constrained by others.

In the public opinion of most American men, liberation is not their concern. Privately, men too may acknowledge feelings of alienation and fragmentation. The fact that some men are vociferously opposed to the liberation of women may suggest the depths of their own feelings of bondage. As men interested in wholeness they must undefensively identify those parts of their lives that seem painfully binding. They may do this by examining the scripts for masculine development assigned by a male-oriented culture. Perhaps ten hours

in the noise and heat of the factory drains men of all compassion for their work or even the family for whom they
have decided to work. Perhaps the commitment to career-
ism needs to be questioned and the preoccupation with
"climbing the ladder" to success, that makes them limit
relationships with their families to a week's summer vaca-
tion, challenged.

Men who seek their own wholeness must acknowledge
the employment, economic, and political discrimination
against women and blacks, in particular, in American society
and the position and privilege generally awarded to white
men as a result of that discrimination. They need to listen to
the language of the culture, to the labels attached to women
and other minorities and consider the effect of these on their
perceptions of minorities. They must begin to suspect, as
alienating, their dependence on positions of authority at
work or at home as these positions sever them from intimacy
with their family members. As men get in touch with the oppression produced by their oppressor status, they must examine their views of women as sexual objects; how do such
views make consideration of female whole persons an im-
possibility?

In a male-oriented society men will undoubtedly find it
difficult to acknowledge themselves as oppressed or to identify with the oppressed because the prevailing hierarchical
way we know the world presupposes leaders and followers,
rich and poor, kings and subjects. Leader groups are less
likely to sense any distortion in their own lives or in the
organization of society than are those who have been
prescribed forever to follow or to remain powerless.
However, by bringing into the open their experiences of
separation and aloneness, born of learning to be competitive
and self-reliant, men may seek another way to be human.

When that occurs men may contact an inner place of
feeling about which they will begin to talk. They may begin
to see their children as people who can teach them about
openness and spontaneity. They may be willing to listen to
the authority of authenticity rather than to position or rank

as it is expressed in people around them. They may encourage their wives to grow personally through studying, taking a job, or volunteering time in social causes. They may share family income responsibilities with their wives so that, as men, they can do volunteer work in child care or public schools, for example. They may reallocate jobs within the home so that both persons have flexibility and choice in routine work.

Men may develop skills they previously assumed to be the sole responsibility of women. They may learn, through more frequent and intense human relationships, that it is *human* to feel strong compassion or to weep. In sexual relations they may learn the excitement of being pursued and cherished as well as pursuing. Only through the acceptance of their fragmentation as human beings can men move to uncover such dormant parts of their inner beings.

The consequences of the movement toward wholeness of women and men are unpredictable, though I suspect a sense of mutuality, of interdependence, will arise as people brush aside the veils of prescribed personality traits and social roles. As whole human beings, women and men can no longer be opposites who have nothing in common. They will discover common needs and share common experiences; they will be alternately teachers and learners together. In their reunion they may know grace and love akin to divine grace and love. They may seek covenant community with other human beings where before they tolerated isolation and superficial exchanges. Through their reunion they will depend on their shared wisdom. In their identification with a common, though differentiated, humanity, they may gradually sense a relationship with the oppressed of the Third World, for example, thus expanding to a global scale one's consciousness of oppression.

The experience of personal wholeness implies relationship with the ground of Being, or God, and propels one into human relationships. As we move toward integrity the realization dawns that we are continually formed by everything and everyone that touches us; likewise, we shape others and the world around us. Our wholeness is rooted in the past and linked with all life in the present. What such a realization points to is inevitable community, a community that theoretically encircles the earth.

Community is commonly referred to in the Old Testament. As the Hebrews responded to the call of God and experienced their chosenness, they rejected their former practices, land, and family ties and wandered together with Yahweh to a new land. The significance of the Hebrew wanderings is not primarily in the location of their physical exile but in their faithfulness to what was happening inside and among them. Old Testament communities, centered in Yahweh, were the reference points from which the members related to and judged the extended culture. The blessing promised to individuals and communities for faithfulness to Yahweh was liberation from bondage.

For modern, technological societies there is nothing which fulfills the same purpose for human beings as the covenant communities of the Israelites. Biological family units used to be the center of life for people, but extended families are obsolete in the 1970s. The church, both in New Testament times and through history, was to be the *koinonia* (sharing community) for believers. But in most places in the half-spent twentieth century the experience of *koinonia* within the institutional church is uncommon, despite pleas for relationships that pull us toward holy personhood and some attempts by church leaders to "program" community-building experiences. Individualism and social conformism run so strongly within most of us that we resist mutuality of community bonds.

Just as personal wholeness leads us toward relationships of interdependence, so corporate liberation from fragmentation or separation occurs only as we find and trust our communities of the exiled. That is, we experience liberation as we deliberately choose to give up (wander from, if you will) the separatist, dichotomized patterns of perceiving and relating, in favor of living out our personal wholeness within non-hierarchical, non-dualistic groups of people who are likewise committed to reclaimed wholeness. Personal wholeness cannot be sustained without relationship with other whole human beings. A liberated, wholistic social order is impossible without union of the oppressed—the rejected, the separated, the alienated, the powerless—who perhaps hear more distinctly the message of a unified Christian gospel based on the life example of Jesus. Thus, it is small communities who know their own and others' oppression that will point the way to the renamed garden for the larger church.

Human beings seeking wholeness and a wholistic view of the world must point the church to its radical[1] Teacher and call it to faith in the renewed creation that Jesus announced and we have only vaguely understood. Women in particular may be able to call to the attention of the church our confusion between faith and theology, *mythos* and *logos;* it is, in part, this confusion upon which our religious beliefs in male supremacy and female subjugation rest.

> The question [where myth ends and theology begins] is crucial because of the painful realization that the Christian myth may have been corrupted by—or confused with—the philosophical views and language in which much of the myth was cast by theologians of the past. When one assents today to so-called Christian teachings, to what extent is one really assenting to discarded notions of reality? For example, in the field of dogma, much of what Christians agree to regarding God and the Trinity seems to be tied into Greek notions of nature, substance, and person. Likewise, in the field of moral theology, the Church (or her theologians) seems to have committed the Christian community to a scheme of ethics based less on revelation than on Greek notions of a static, defined, and closed human nature.[2]

What the Christian church has done by separating faith from theology, the *mythos* from the *logos,* is to cut us off from the essence of the Gospel and to remove us from revelation that comes continually into human consciousness and through human relationships. This separation has permitted our idolatry of rationalism, and it has not consistently challenged the questionable assumption that principally through theology one understands the essence of Christ.

Jesus stands in sharp contrast to the Greek notions of

nature, substance, and person; his ethics do not arise from belief in a static, definable, and closed human nature. Through Jesus *mythos* and *logos* are unified. *Logos* means word, which in philosophic terms is connected with idea. The *logos* of the universe, the great "I am" personified in Yahweh by the Hebrews, became flesh in the incarnation of Jesus. In relationship, made possible by the incarnation of Jesus, the Father (Mother) and Spirit of the Trinity were brought to life. Divinity erupted in humanity. Humanity carried divinity within it. The great Word became flesh and continues to be vitalized at every birth. Through the *mythos,* the existential revelation of the *logos,* the Word, was energized; and the people experienced the "I am" among them and sensed its power within them.

A return to the Christian myth, the story of Jesus' earthbound ministry, helps us to understand the paradoxes of wholeness that he revealed. In his revelation dichotomies were overcome; hierarchies became meaningless; caste and class distinctions were ignored. Liberation and reconciliation are the messages and the experiences of the gospel that challenge our current commitments to hierarchies, caste and class, fragmented world views, a static notion of human nature, and closed social systems. As covenanted communities bear witness to a renamed garden and take seriously the revelation of Jesus, they will (1) give centrality to the female-male union both as symbol of wholeness and as actual model for human relationships; (2) reveal a God of wholeness; (3) reunite spirituality and sexuality; and (4) devote themselves to the liberation of all the oppressed. What this might mean in practice for the churches of Christ we will examine in the following paragraphs.

Why should the Christian church place at the center of its teachings the united female and male when throughout most of its history the church has ignored the relationship of woman and man except as it preached doctrines of male lordship and female servitude? We may begin to answer this question by referring to a symbol dominant in both the Old and New Testaments: the marriage symbol. For many associated with the church, the analogy of the relationship between God and Israel or Christ and the church with human marriage is just another way of supporting male power and female weakness. What they see in the symbolic representation is God's "masculine" salvation of Israel and Christ's powerful, one-sided redemption of the church. If we permit our vision to stop with such fragmented interpretation of the marriage symbol used throughout the Bible, we not only fail to understand the implications of the symbol for our own human relationships, but we teach an unbiblical doctrine of the church.

What can we learn about the nature of Jesus, his mission, and the potential of marriage through the use of a human, earth-tied relationship as symbol for something associated with divinity? Is the bride image of the church to be interpreted as Christ's inferior? Or does our historic cultural view of bride as subject of her husband render insight into the biblical symbol of the church as the bride of Christ impossible?

Those of us who have been taught to hate our sexuality, our fleshly and emotional lives, and who have internalized the archaic cultural attitudes about woman and marriage, interpret Christ's reference to the church as bride as a supreme "put down." The use by the writers of the Gospel of the female/male covenant known as marriage to describe Christ's relationship with the church, his bride, is a revelation of the nature of the new covenant in Christ. Jesus embodies in union the human and the divine. The new covenant expressed through his incarnation is not solely divine; it is reunion through redemptive relationship of the divine and the human. Neither a bride nor a groom is sinless, Christ was not exclusively divine.

Both a bride and a groom are finite, and each may be a grievous sinner. Yet the marriage relationship may provide a glimpse of the kingdom of heaven through the mutual acceptance and forgiveness experienced in the marriage covenant. So it is with Christ and his bride, the church. Individually judged, members of a group may be serious sinners, but when they come into a relationship of forgiveness and wholeness with Christ and others, transformation occurs, and divinity is disclosed.

The nuptial analogy is chosen deliberately to reveal the ultimate significance of the human-divine covenant expressed through Christ. Jesus is human-divine, an incarnation of God-human. He was not Greek pure spirit, absolute divinity, abstract idea outside the reach of earth. He was of the flesh, acquainted with bribery and debauchery, related to the despised and rejected, and was despised and rejected himself. In this earthly form, through relationship with God and human beings, he takes on the divine. His church is a gathering of publicans and prodigal sons, but through relationship with him it is divine. An unbiblical doctrine of the church removes the church from the earth, from direct involvement in the affairs of human beings, from redemptive relationship with Jesus. Such a church may be described as an abstraction of the Incarnation. In such a view there is no covenant relationship, no marriage, no union of the human and the divine.

From the biblical use of marriage as a symbol of the divine-human union we may find at work in our own female-male relationships the energizing of the divine, that mystery that occurs between persons and transcends their finiteness. We are "saved," as it were, from isolation and separation by the covenant we accept for union. As the church gives central significance to the female/male union as symbol of the divine/human union, all our earthly relationships are affected. The "marriage" between two human beings or among humanity is the entry of the divine into our midst.

The importance of the union of female and male has been pointed out by Beatriz Melano Couch in her analysis of Jesus' encounter with the Samaritan who asked him for the "living water," generally interpreted as the symbol of the new life. In John 4:16 he sent her home saying, "Go, call your husband, and come here." Couch raises the following questions about that meeting:

What does it mean that Christ is definitely asking man and woman to drink of the living water together? Could not it be that Christ is calling men and women together to partake of the New Humanity as a unity, the basic unity of God's creation. . . .[3]

Only as the church, or small communities within the church, accepts the union of female and male as symbol of the new humanity can it be about the business of liberation.

As the church begins to understand the unity of female and male, the two most basic polarities of the fallen creation, it will understand God as wholeness. As woman and man take unto themselves some of their so-called antithetical qualities and are redeemed and reunited through that process, our beliefs about God will be drastically affected. If we see divinity in female as well as male form, we will no longer be able to pray to or preach about "father" God alone. Openly and regularly we will be able to identify with God as unity of female and male; we will understand from our own hurts the weeping of God, the compassion as well as the majesty ascribed to God.

As we sense the divine in human beings we will be less able to move God "out there" beyond human experience; instead God will be sought within ourselves, in others, and in the midst of the interaction of our communities that make covenant with God and one another. It will become increasingly difficult to view ourselves as the only "elected" of the children of the earth; thus, the oppressed will become sisters and brothers of a shared parent God.

By studying history and archaeology, religion and sociology, we will understand how other places and people have viewed the sacred in their lives and how such views can expand our experiences of the divine. We may be surprised at reports like Elizabeth Gould Davis':

Since 1966 detailed reports have been made on three prehistoric towns in Anatolia: Mersin, Hacilar, and Catal Huyuk. And in all of them the message is clear and unequivocal: ancient society was *gynocratic* and its deity feminine. . . . In the golden age of Judeo-Christian myth, paradise was a land "flowing with milk and honey." And it may surprise the patriarchal Jews and Christians of today to learn that milk and honey both symbolize feminine rule. . . .[4]

When we acknowledge foreign interpretations of the sacred, of the ordering of the universe, we become more sensitive to the complexity of human beings and the magnificence of all Being. Narrow religious, tribal, and national loyalties will gradually be replaced with a universal consciousness that simultaneously enlarges our God. Such changes will have profound potential for turning nationalism toward world community.

In understanding God as wholeness we will discover expressions of Being in the material world of nature and within our own experiences of waking, thinking, working with our hands, making love, reproducing life, and knowing death. When we worship a whole God, no longer will we be able easily to abstract or spiritualize our concrete existences but will find holiness in them that may deepen our knowledge of the spiritual.

Out of the psychological, intellectual, and spiritual mutuality of the sexes and from knowledge of God as wholeness should come the reunification of spirituality and sexuality within each human being. However, such reunion is impossible when feelings of shame or disgust about one's body, rooted in a hierarchical division of life into higher (spirit) and lower (nature) categories, dominate. The Christian church's role historically has been to accentuate the division between spirit and body.

In the renamed garden, like that described in the Song of Solomon, there is no shame of the body or of the physical passion one experiences for the beloved. Neither woman nor man can be exploited when sexuality is part of the whole being of oneself and one's partner. Exploitation arises from hostility, hostility felt toward one's own body or from the desire to possess the body of one's mate. In the garden in the Song the mutuality and union that female and male know physically is part of the kinship they know together with nature.

Sexuality is not a separate compartment of human life; it is a radiance pervading every human relationship, but assuming a particular intensity at certain points. Conversely, we might say that sexuality is a special mode or degree of the total intercourse of man and nature.[5]

Much of our confusion about our own sexual identities, of our concern about our sexual performance, encouraged by Western emphasis on sex techniques and methods, and of our feeling betrayed in our sex acts, arises, Alan Watts suggests, from our world view. So long as we compartmentalize our own beings and separate ourselves from the other creatures and processes of nature we will never know intimacy, spontaneity, and union with others. Instead we respond to one another as antagonists, as objects for one another's grasp, and we live in nature as its masters or enemies.

Perhaps for the reunion of sexuality and spirituality to occur we will need to be more contemplative and less active in our relationship with nature and in sexual relationships. Just as through meditation in nature something of its power and beauty creeps into us without our willing it, so in the quiet consideration of one's beloved the physical signs of passion arrive naturally and unforced. They are stimulated by the appreciation of her or his whole being beside which one rests in awe and devotion.

Such a contemplative approach to sexual exchanges, including or excluding intercourse, is radically different from the instruction one receives from a church and a culture that repress human sexuality, thereby making it a hostile exchange. Human relationships are potentially transformed from manipulative, grasping confrontations to mutual experiences of spontaneous intimacy. It seems likely that through this kind of transformed human relationship one comes closer to understanding the essence of the spirit, of divine compassion.

The above means of creating changed ways of living with each other and of understanding ourselves suggest ultimately a new world view. It is a wholistic world view bearing some similarities to Chinese Taoism and strongly reflected in the incarnation of Jesus. The most important difference between Western thought and Chinese philosophy can be explained in this manner

> ... there [are] no categories of Chinese thought corresponding to spirit and nature as we [in the West] understand them. Here was a culture in which the conflict between spirit and nature hardly existed, a culture where the most "naturalistic" painting and poetry were precisely the most "spiritual" of its art forms.[6]

Many of us reared on a Western approach to life and within a religious institution that elevates the spiritual dimension of life are not at home in our bodies or in nature. We may argue that our appreciation of sexual attractiveness or prowess, that our frank interest in perfecting sex techniques and sexual adjustment, that our expenditures to adorn the body, that our use of nature in our recreation are all signs of the ease with which we live with our bodies and nature. Yet in all the above interests we stand apart from that which we believe we enjoy or admire. We are not one with the whole being of another so long as we view sex as a separate "act"; we are not one with ourselves when we feel we need to dress up or make up what we are naturally; we are not one with nature when "doing" something in or to nature is the extent of our relationship with it.

In all these expressions we are subjects usurping power over other objects or separated aspects of our own beings. We view both the flesh and nature as lower dimensions of life needing the control of the spirit. It is out of the historic rejection of wholeness that our personal alienation is born and our social relationships become oppressive.

The task of the church in cultivating a renamed garden is to teach and preach about the great separations created and encountered by Western human beings. In the church we will examine our racism, our nation's imperialism, and our personal and corporate sexism *in addition* to reading Galatians 3:28 and singing "In Christ There Is No East or West." We will seek the plumb line by which to measure our lives. The reason for studying our own participation in oppression becomes obvious when we consider that Christ's message of wholeness and liberation from all sorts of bondage—slavery, epilepsy, blindness, prostitution, power—

has been present for us for two thousand years. Despite its existence and our profession of belief in that message, we often cling to separations and bondage.

If small communities experience reunion in all areas of life—the personal, interpersonal, religious, and social—they can become models for the larger church and society. Perhaps then we will more accurately understand what Jesus meant when he suggested that we live *in* the world but should not be *of* it. There is urgency for whole females and males to live *in* the world and to relate mutually rather than hierarchically. The time is urgent for us to declare by our actions our unwillingness to participate in systems that oppress human life. As such declarations are made by individuals and communities, the institutional church will not be able to live as an oppressor but will be transformed from within into a potential liberator. As churches accept the call to liberate, they will be required to seek social justice. They will evaluate decisions and actions of other social institutions—schools, businesses, government agencies—and encourage them to change those policies or practices that deny wholeness to individuals, fluidity of roles and interdependence between the sexes, and recognition of divinity in humanity.

The church as a cultivator of the renamed garden must offer its friends and critics options for living outside the prevailing culture. Thus, it should find itself making choices in favor of:

1. simplified, nonmaterialistic, ecological life-styles;
2. economic reforms that weaken class and caste distinctions;
3. government agencies and representatives that encourage alert citizenship rather than mindless authoritarianism;
4. prison, labor, and education reforms that base their institutional existences on serving human life;
5. legal, medical, and mental aid services for all people;
6. reevaluation by women and men of professionalism that exploits or devalues the nonprofessional;
7. development of a world-consciousness that erodes

nationalism as the highest loyalty of people and creates a universalism that includes the Third World of which, as the affluent of the world, we know little.

If small covenanted communities took seriously some of the above suggestions, we might find ourselves approaching a jubilee. In fact, it is to a jubilee, as described in the Old and New Testaments, that liberated women and men need to call the church if we are to move deliberately to a new order.

In Exodus 22 and 23 and Leviticus 25 we find reference to a sabbatical year for the Hebrews. The seventh year was a year of rest for the land and is described in Exodus 23:10-11:

> For six years you shall sow your land and gather in its yield; but the seventh year you shall let it rest and lie fallow, that the poor of your people may eat; and what they leave the wild beasts may eat. You shall do likewise with your vineyard.

After forty-nine years, on the fiftieth year, the jubilee was proclaimed, as we find in Leviticus 25:8-12:

> And you shall count seven weeks of years, seven times seven years, so that the time of the seven weeks of years shall be to you forty-nine years. Then you shall send abroad the loud trumpet on the tenth day of the seventh month; on the day of atonement you shall send abroad the trumpet throughout all your land. And you shall hallow the fiftieth year, and proclaim liberty throughout the land to all its inhabitants; it shall be a jubilee for you, when each of you shall return to his property and each of you shall return to his family. A jubilee shall that fiftieth year be to you; in it you shall neither sow, nor reap what grows of itself, nor gather the grapes from the undressed vines. For it is a jubilee; you shall eat what it yields out of the field.

The four prescriptions of the sabbath and the jubilee years were: "(1) leaving the soil fallow; (2) the remission of debts; (3) the liberation of slaves; (4) the return to each individual of his family's property."[7] In both the sabbath years and the jubilee year human beings were reminded that they were not absolute owners of the soil; they held their property in trust with God. Both celebrations, and particularly the jubilee, were occasions of thanksgiving; during both one was recalled to faith in God and unity with all the people of the land. All were reminded that no one possessed anything by inherent right.

In *The Politics of Jesus,* John Howard Yoder suggests that Jesus proclaimed the inauguration of the jubilee year. He supports his assertion with the following reasons. First, the Jews in Jesus' time were practicing the sabbath prescription to keep the soil fallow. Second, the Lord's Prayer announces the remission of debts by God toward human beings and between human beings. The verb *aphiemi* means erase, remit, or liberate and such remission is to be given in the way God has erased human debts. Yoder explains the prayer.

> It means "the time has come for the faithful people to abolish all the debts which tie the poor ones of Israel, for your debts toward God are also wiped away (for that is the gospel, the good news)." . . . Jesus was establishing a strict equation between the practice of the jubilee and the grace of God. He who was not legalist at any other point, and who was ready without hesitation to pardon prostitutes and disreputable people, was nonetheless extremely strict upon one point: "only he who practices grace can receive grace. The *aphesis* of God toward you becomes vain if you do not practice aphesis toward your brethren."[8]

Third, in the parable of the unfaithful steward (Luke 16:1ff.), Jesus illustrates how liberation from bondage to another person is realized. The steward in the parable had cheated the sharecroppers by extorting sums in excess of the amounts owed his master, and he cheated the master by falsifying records. When his dishonesty was discovered he

> " . . . restored to his debtors the unjust excess of the debt which they were supposed to owe him." . . . Certainly such a decision would only aggravate the insolvency of the steward. It would reduce him to poverty. But in acting this way he acquired genuine wealth, namely the gratitude and the friendship of his former victims . . . This is what Jesus calls the joys of the kingdom of God . . . ' Practice the jubilee which I am announcing. By liberating others from their debts to you, liberate yourself from the bonds which keep you from being ready for the kingdom of God."[9]

Fourth, Jesus directed the people in Luke 12:30-37 to sell what they had and to give it as alms. Out of the context of jubilee that advice has been troublesome for Christians since it was offered. It was Jesus' call to redistribute capital. If one gives a token of one's income "this is not righteousness, goodness and good faith";[10] what is important is the redistribution, through compassion, of capital.

> Such a redistribution of capital, accomplished every fifty years by faithfulness to the righteous will of God and in the expectation of the kingdom, would today be nothing utopian. Many bloody revolutions would have been avoided if the Christian church had shown herself more respectful than Israel was of the jubilee dispositions contained in the law of Moses.[11]

If the women's movement is to move us toward a united humanity and social structures that do not imitate the fallen creation, it could begin by proclaiming a jubilee. Such a proclamation would require that we reconsider the meaning of faithfulness to a God of wholeness, a Mother-Father God, a God within us who acts through us to reveal new life and forms. Although the jubilee was never realized in Jesus' time, it has power for us as symbol for reorienting our world views and reordering our lives.

The garden that we have produced in the fallen creation has been overworked. From it we Americans have harvested two thirds of the world's wealth; from our overuse the soil needs rest, and from our relentless quest for profits we need a pause. Our experience during the 1977 winter with frigid weather and decreased natural gas supplies illustrates our over-consumption and the finiteness of resources. The drought some scientists predicted for the summer of 1977 by reading sunspots, also should move us to reconsider our dependence on nature. We may, for physical survival, need to practice the biblical jubilee by planting and harvesting in good years and preserving supplies for the years when nature restores itself.

The results of keeping a jubilee year are unpredictable, but we can imagine what honoring a jubilee might mean in changing the present values by which we live. Just as among the Israelites the jubilee was a community festival, so keeping the jubilee in our own time would best be done in community. Jubilee is a call to the persons in a whole community to reappraise their relationships. Reasons for being in community become obvious as we look at what the jubilee might require of us.

First, the jubilee would offer us the opportunity to cease our labor and to measure our lives. It would give us time to contemplate and act upon the ideal. The jubilee might present the occasion for a community (of several families) to make an exodus to a new location. Old patterns of work and consumption are more easily avoided in new surroundings. However, a small group could decide to stay placed but to practice drastically altered work patterns. Each unit could contribute, for example, money from part-time work for the support of the whole group. Where savings or assets are such that a steady income is unnecessary, the group might decide that all should rest from business as usual. Where men have been the sole or major wage earners and women have cared for the home and family, roles might be reversed so that each could experience the other's responsibilities.

The group might decide to support one family equipped to share agricultural/nutritional skills in a country like Bangladesh. It would surely encourage participation in movements to promote global social justice, to protect the environment, to denuclearize the planet. All our imagination should be applied to thinking of ways we might stand in the shoes of others and stand on behalf of others. We cannot measure our lives seriously without looking at our relation to the total world. We need to examine our lives within the narrow contexts of biological family, or village, or denomination, or social class, or nation—to see how these may violate the biblical understanding of wholeness. We dare not avoid the New Testament question, "Who is my brother? Who is my sister?" And Christ gives us a clear example of how to answer it.

Second, the jubilee would be a time of "letting go." Self-reliance would be replaced by interdependency. Lending and borrowing would replace individual acquisitiveness. People would decide to close revolving charge accounts and to postpone building additions to their homes or buying fashionable clothes. No land or house or boat would seem to belong to anyone by inherent right; therefore, churches might act as holding companies of such possessions during the jubilee. Churches might encourage bankers to lower or declare a twelve-month moratorium on mortgage payments in the spirit of *aphesis*. Leaders of businesses might remit the debts of the poor in the same spirit. In all the transactions of holding property, erasing debts, or lowering payments, churches might act as a third party guaranteeing the agreement.

Churches would lead the way in re-evaluating their investments with national and multinational corporations. They would accept responsibility to hold corporations accountable for practicing social justice, insuring environmental safety, and advancing political openness and equity among all peoples of the globe. When persuasion proves ineffective, they would consider nonviolent pressures such as economic boycott. They would question business and governmental leaders about the morality of defending economic growth when human needs go unmet in vast areas of the world.

Third, the jubilee would permit us to evaluate our relationships with one another. Women and men would examine the bondage we have forced upon one another by rigid sex stereotypes and reconsider the meaning of personhood. Through remission of one another's transgressions (manipulating or allowing manipulation, for example) we could receive genuine wealth, " . . . the gratitude and friendship of . . . former victims."[12]

In the jubilee we would have time to listen to one another, to explore ourselves, to learn new skills or ways of expression from each other. Time could be spent together making things with our hands, studying art or literature, keeping journals or writing essays, playing with each other and the young. Children in the jubilee year would become people because there would be time to know and to enjoy them. They could teach adults faith and freedom; adults could interpret history and current events and share wisdom. Parents and children might go to school together in a classroom or system honoring the jubilee. Mothers and fathers could share their special interests or talents by being instructors; and children could know the delight in learning with their parents' immediate participation.

Fourth, the jubilee would be a time of redistribution of capital. In our time such redistribution would have long-lasting psychological, as well as material, consequences. For example, a single family might appraise its material wealth and study how that wealth is shared among the family members. Does each person receive a fair share of the capital? Are those with more control of the wealth or responsibility for acquiring it granted greater power in family transactions? What would happen psychologically to those members with little or no capital if they received a fair portion?

The family might also evaluate its status comparatively with the local, national, or global community. In what position are they in comparison with families on welfare, with families of migrant farmers, with lawyer or teacher families, with Pakistani peasants? If a family or community decided, as an outgrowth of jubilee evaluation, to redistribute its capital beyond the immediate group, the members might decide to give portions of their capital to a specific person or group. The church could act as a distributive agency for those who desire to divide their capital more equitably. As such an agency the church would be continually examining the needs of people and the structures that prohibit social justice.

Proclamation of a jubilee is a radical step. It forces us into relationships we usually avoid; the poor and the rich might move toward interdependency; women and men might have flexible territories of interest and responsibility; families might extend compassion beyond their near neighbors; the church might embrace sinners and saints; in the name of a Mother-Father God it might call women and men into the total mission of the church.

Jubilee gives us time to perceive the world, not from positions of power or prestige, but from experiences of humility and unity with others. Because of our personal reevaluation within a global context we might be moved toward whole personhood and a wholistic world view. Will anything short of a temporary pause in business as usual permit us ultimately to be liberated human beings who have a sense of communal personhood and who are capable of creating a new communal social ethic?

Perhaps only as we allow ourselves to consider the blessing of jubilee will we know ourselves and one another as part of " . . . the seamless unity of nature . . . "[13] that survives all time and transcends all cultures and nations. We are called by a sense of the seamless unity around and within us to give up our bondage as separated females and males and to extend solidarity *(mishpat)* and integrity *(sedequah)* to the human family in a renamed garden.

Into My Own

Read the Exodus 22—23 and Leviticus 25 accounts of the sabbatical and jubilee years.

Make a list of all the reasons a jubilee proclamation would not be practical.

Make a list of all the reasons you believe it might have value.

What would you be about during a jubilee?

Consider forming a *koinonia* group of friends with whom you would try to envision a renamed garden. Permit this experience to be faith-building and heart-sharing.

NOTES

Introduction

[1] *Deus ex machina* is a Latin phrase used to depict a god who artifically or improbably intervenes to affect the course of events. Such a god is manipulative and machine-like.

[2] Alan Watts, *Nature, Man and Woman* (New York: Vintage Books, 1970), p. 9.

Chapter 1

[1] Aileen S. Kraditor, ed., *Up From the Pedestal* (Chicago: Quadrangle Press, 1968), p. 109.

[2] *Ibid.*

[3] Casey Miller and Kate Swift, "One Small Step for Genkind," *New York Times Magazine* (April 16, 1972), p. 36.

[4] *Ibid.*, p. 100.

[5] *Ibid.*, p. 101.

[6] Steve Engle, "I See a New World Coming," copyrighted by Steve Engle and the La Verne, California, Church of the Brethren.

[7] Miller and Swift, *loc. cit.*, p. 101.

[8] *Ibid.*, p. 106.

[9] The terms "low-church" and "high-church" referred traditionally to two branches of the Anglican Church. Today low-church applies broadly to those groups stressing simplicity in religious forms and a more evangelical doctrine than the high-church. The term high-church is used for those groups emphasizing rituals, sacraments, the priesthood, and orthodox doctrine.

[10] Miriam Crist and Tilda Norberg, "Sex-Role Stereotyping" in Sarah B. Doely, ed., *Women's Liberation and the Church* (New York: Association Press, 1970), p. 119.

[11] *Ibid.*

[12] *Ibid.*

[13] Lou Ann Talcott, "Sex Role Stereotyping in the Church of the Brethren Encounter Series for Preschool Children" (independent research available from Church of the Brethren General Offices).

[14] *Ibid.*, pp. 5-6.

[15] Donald J. Selby, *Introduction to the New Testament* (New York: Macmillan Co., 1971), p. 386.

[16] Anna Mow, *The Secret of Married Love* (New York: J. B. Lippincott Co., 1970), p. 21.

[17] *Ibid.*, p. 72.

[18] *Ibid.*, p. 21.

Chapter 2

[1] Neoplatonism refers to a school of philosophy, founded in the third century A.D., that incorporated the ideas of Plato with the ethical concepts typical of Judaism and Christianity and with the mysticism of the Near East.

[2] Rosemary Reuther, "Mother Earth and the Megamachine," *Christianity and Crisis,* XXXI, 21 (December 13, 1971), p. 267.

[3] Alan Watts, *Nature, Man and Woman* (New York: Vintage Books, 1970, 1958), p. 98.

[4] William Graham Cole, *Sex and Love in the Bible* (New York: Association Press, 1959), p. 221.

[5] *Ibid.,* p. 222.

[6] *Ibid.,* pp. 228-229.

[7] *Ibid.,* p. 235.

[8] Phyllis Trible, "Depatriarchalizing in Biblical Interpretation," *Journal of the American Academy of Religion* XLI/1 (March 1973), p. 33.

[9] Three characteristics of ancient covenantal communities were: a common history; a shared set of norms; a unifying ritual.

[10] Barbara Boynton, "James Prescott: Touching," *Intellectual Digest* (March 1974), pp. 6-10.

Chapter 3

[1] Elizabeth Janeway, *Man's World, Woman's Place: A Study in Social Mythology* (New York: Morrow, 1971), p. 45.

[2] The word *man* appearing in quotations throughout this book should be understood to mean woman as well.

[3] Jerome Bruner, "Myth and Identity," in Henry A. Murray's *Myth and Mythmaking* (New York: George Braziller, 1960), p. 276.

[4] Russell Barta, "Demythologizing Theology," *America,* Vol. 126, No. 5 (February 5, 1972), p. 118.

[5] As quoted by Edith Hamilton, *Mythology* (Boston: Little, Brown and Co., 1942), p. 78.

[6] Sam Keen, "Man and Myth: A Conversation With Joseph Campbell," *Psychology Today,* V (July 1971), p. 91.

[7] Campbell, *op. cit.,* p. 28.

[8] Phyllis Trible, "Depatriarchalizing in Biblical Interpretation," *Journal of the American Academy of Religion* XLI/1 (March 1973), p. 31.

[9] *Ibid.,* pp. 31 and 34.

[10] *Ibid.* p. 34.

[11] *Ibid.,* p. 36.

[12] *Ibid.,* pp. 37-38.

[13] *Ibid.,* p. 40.

[14] *Ibid.,* p. 41.

[15] *Ibid.*

[16] *Ibid.*

[17] As quoted in *ibid.,* p. 43.

[18] *Ibid.,* p. 44.

[19] *Ibid.,* p. 46.

[20] *Ibid.,* p. 48.

[21] Margaret Mead, *Sex and Temperament in Three Primitive Societies* (New York: Dell Publishing Co., Inc., 1935, 1950, 1963), p. 16.

[22] *Ibid.,* pp. 17-18.

[23] Alan Watts, *Nature, Man and Woman* (New York: Vintage Books, 1970, 1958), p. 179.

[24] *Ibid.*

Chapter 4

[1] This concept is elaborated in Reuel Howe, *The Miracle of Dialogue* (New York: Seabury Press, 1963).

[2] Paulo Freire, *The Pedagogy of the Oppressed* (New York: Herder & Herder, 1970), p. 76.

[3] Sam Keen, "Man and Myth: A Conversation With Joseph Campbell," *Psychology Today,* V (July 1971), p. 91.

[4] Freire, *op. cit.,* pp. 10-11.

[5] Robin Morgan, ed., "Barbarous Rituals," *Sisterhood Is Powerful* (New York: Vintage Press, 1970), p. 164.

Chapter 5

[1] Erich Fromm, *Escape From Freedom* (New York: Holt, Rinehart and Winston, 1941), p. 140.

[2] Rollo May, *Love and Will* (New York: W. W. Norton & Co., Inc., 1969), pp. 123-129.

[3] Sidney Jourard, *Disclosing Man to Himself* (Princeton: D. Van Nostrand Co., Inc., 1968), p. 47.

[4] Susan Sontag, "The Double Standard of Aging," *Saturday Review of the Society* (October 1972), p. 34.

[5] *Ibid.,* p. 35.

[6] The reader is referred to Chapters 2 and 7 for discussion of the purpose of creation.

[7] Beatriz Melano Couch, "A Key to the Understanding of the New Humanity," *Church and Society,* (September-October 1972), p. 43.

Chapter 6

[1] Ellen Willis, "Economic Reality and the Limits of Feminism," *Ms.,* (June 1973), p. 91.

[2] *Ibid.,* p. 90.

[3] *Ibid.*

[4] David Coute, *Frantz Fanon* (New York: Viking Press, 1970).

[5] Elizabeth Janeway, *Man's World, Woman's Place: A Study in Social Mythology* (New York: Morrow, 1971), pp. 14-21.

[6] Eleanor Flexnor, *Century of Struggle* (New York: Atheneum, 1971), p. 288.

[7] Thomas J. Cottle, "A Middle American Marriage," *Harper's Magazine,* (February 1973), p. 68.

[8] Karen Horney, "The Distrust Between the Sexes," in *Feminine Psychology,* Harold Kelman, ed. (New York: W. W. Norton & Co., Inc., 1967), p. 112.

[9] *Ibid.,* p. 115.

[10] Karen Horney, "The Dread of Woman," *op. cit.,* p. 135.

[11] Karen Horney, "The Distrust Between the Sexes," *op. cit.,* p. 113.

[12] Anne Sexton in *All My Pretty Ones* (New York: Houghton Mifflin, 1961, 1962).

[13] Marie Ratagick, "Two American Welfare Mothers," *Ms.,* (June 1973), pp. 76-77.

[14] Alexander Auerbach, "Women Sue Insurance Companies," Fort Wayne, Indiana, *News-Sentinel* (February 9, 1974).

[15] Paulo Freire, *The Pedagogy of the Oppressed* (New York: Herder & Herder, 1970), p. 28.

[16] *Ibid.,* p. 73.

[17] Radical (from Latin *radix*) is to be understood as root, the original, the basic or innate nature of something described. Hence, the potential for radical union is carried in the roots of each human being. Radical union is the innate union for which, I assert, each organism reaches. Opposed to radical union is traditionally casual, superficial exchange between persons.

[18] Paulo Freire, *op. cit.,* p. 42.

Chapter 7

[1] Radical is used here as it was in Chapter 6.

[2] Russell Barta, "Demythologizing Theology," *America,* CXXVI, No. 5 (February 5, 1972), p. 120.

[3] Beatriz Melano Couch, "A Key to the Understanding of the New Humanity," *Church and Society,* September-October 1972, pp. 47-48.

[4] Elizabeth Gould Davis, *The First Sex* (Baltimore: Penguin Books, Inc., 1972), pp. 77-79.

[5] Alan Watts, *Nature, Man and Woman* (New York: Vintage Books, 1958, 1970), pp. 189-190.

[6] *Ibid.,* p. xi.

[7] John Howard Yoder, *The Politics of Jesus* (Grand Rapids: William B. Eerdmans Publishing Co., 1972), p. 64.

[8] *Ibid.,* p. 67.

[9] *Ibid.,* p. 73.

[10] *Ibid.,* p. 76

[11] *Ibid.,* pp. 76-77.

[12] *Ibid.,* p. 73.

[13] Alan Watts, *op. cit.,* p. 9.

SELECTED BIBLIOGRAPHY

Books

Beard, Mary R. *Woman as Force in History*. New York: Collier Books, 1946, 1962, 1971.

Berne, Eric. *Games People Play*. New York: Grove Press, 1964.

Bird, Caroline. *Born Female: The High Cost of Keeping Women Down*. New York: McKay Co., Inc., 1968.

Bolle, Kees W. *The Freedom of Man in Myth*. Nashville: Vanderbilt University Press, 1968.

Campbell, Joseph. *The Hero of a Thousand Faces*. New York: Meridian Books, 1956.

_____. *The Masks of God: Primitive Mythology*. New York: Viking Press, 1959.

_____. *Myths to Live By*. New York: Viking Press, 1972.

Caute, David. *Frantz Fanon*. New York: Viking Press, 1970.

Cervantes. *Don Quixote*. New York: Viking Press, 1949, 1950, 1951.

Cole, William Graham. *Sex and Love in the Bible*. New York: Association Press, 1959.

_____. *Sex in Christianity and Psychoanalysis*. New York: Oxford University Press, 1955.

Cooke, Joanne; Bunch-Weeks, Charlotte; and Morgan, Robin, eds. *The New Women: An Anthology of Women's Liberation*. Greenwich, Conn.: Fawcett Publications, Inc., 1970.

Daly, Mary. *Beyond God the Father: Toward a Philosophy of Women's Liberation*. Boston: Beacon Press, 1973.

_____. *The Church and the Second Sex*. New York: Harper & Row, 1968.

Davis, Elizabeth Gould. *The First Sex*. Baltimore: Penguin Books, Inc., 1971, 1973.

de Beauvoir, Simone. *The Second Sex*. New York: Alfred A. Knopf, Inc., 1949, 1953.

de Riencourt, Amaury. *Sex and Power in History*. New York: Dell Publishing Co., 1974.

Deutsch, Helene. *The Psychology of Women: Girlhood.* New York: Grune & Stratton, 1944.

——————. *The Psychology of Women: Motherhood.* New York: Grune & Stratton, 1944.

Doely, Sarah Bentley, ed. *Women's Liberation and the Church.* New York: Association Press, 1970.

Dreifus, Claudia. *Woman's Fate: Raps From a Feminist Consciousness-Raising Group.* New York: Bantam Books, 1973.

Dudley, Guilford, III. *The Recovery of Christian Myth.* Philadelphia: Westminster Press, 1967.

Eliade, Mircea. *Myths, Dreams, and Mysteries.* New York: Harper & Brothers Publishers, 1960.

Erikson, Erik. *Childhood and Society.* New York: Norton & Co., Inc., 1950, 1963.

Ermarth, Margaret. *Adam's Fractured Rib.* Philadelphia: Fortress Press, 1970.

Fanon, Frantz. *A Dying Colonialism.* New York: Grove Press, Inc., 1965.

——————. *The Wretched of the Earth.* New York: Grove Press, Inc., 1963.

Flexner, Eleanor. *Century of Struggle.* New York: Atheneum, 1971.

Freire, Paulo. *The Pedagogy of the Oppressed.* New York: Herder & Herder, 1970.

Fromm, Erich. *The Art of Loving.* New York: Bantam, 1956.

——————. *Escape From Freedom.* New York: Holt, Rinehart & Winston, 1941.

——————. *The Revolution of Hope.* New York: Harper & Row, 1968.

——————. *The Sane Society.* New York: Holt, Rinehart & Winston, 1955.

Harkness, Georgia. *Women in Church and Society.* Nashville: Abingdon Press, 1972.

Harrelson, Walter. *Interpreting the Old Testament.* New York: Holt, Rinehart, Winston, 1964.

Harris, Thomas A. *I'm O.K., You're O.K.,* New York: Harper & Row, 1967.

Horney, Karen. *Feminine Psychology.* Edited by Harold Kelman. New York: W. W. Norton & Co., Inc., 1967.

Jacobi, Jolande. *The Psychology of C. G. Jung.* New Haven: Yale University Press, 1943, 1951.

James, Muriel, and Jongeword, Dorothy. *Born to Win.* Philippines: Addison-Wesley Publishing Co., Inc., 1971.

Janeway, Elizabeth. *Man's World, Woman's Place: A Study in Social Mythology.* New York: William Morrow & Co., Inc., 1971.

Jourard, Sidney M. *Disclosing Man to Himself.* Princeton: Van Nostrand Co., Inc., 1968.

Jung, C. G. *Memories, Dreams, Reflections.* Recorded and edited by Aniela Jaffe. New York: Vintage, 1963.

_____. *Modern Man in Search of a Soul.* New York: Harcourt, Brace, & Co., 1933.

Keen, Sam. *To a Dancing God.* New York: Harper & Row, 1970.

Kraditor, Aileen S., ed. *Up From the Pedestal.* Chicago: Quadrangle Press, 1968.

Mace, David. *The Christian Response to the Sexual Revolution.* Nashville: Abingdon Press, 1970.

May, Rollo. *Love and Will.* New York: Norton & Co., Inc., 1969.

_____. *Power and Innocence.* New York: Norton & Co., Inc., 1972.

Mead, Margaret. *Sex and Temperament in Three Primitive Societies.* New York: Dell Publishing Co., Inc., 1935, 1950, 1963.

Millett, Kate. *Sexual Politics.* New York: Doubleday & Co., 1970.

Montagu, Ashley. *The Natural Superiority of Woman.* New York: Collier Books, 1952, 1953, 1968.

Morgan, Robin, ed. *Sisterhood Is Powerful.* New York: Vintage, 1970.

Mow, Anna B. *The Secret of Married Love.* New York: J. B. Lippincott Co., 1970.

Murray, Henry A., ed. *Myth and Mythmaking.* New York: George Braziller, 1960.

Reuther, Rosemary. *Liberation Theology.* New York: Paulist Press, 1972.

Scanzoni, Letha, and Hardesty, Nancy. *All We're Meant to Be.* Waco, Texas: Word Books, 1974.

Selby, Donald J. *Introduction to the New Testament.* New York: Macmillan Co., 1971.

Sexton, Anne. *All My Pretty Ones.* New York: Houghton Mifflin, 1961, 1962.

Sochen, June, ed. *The New Feminism in Twentieth-Century America.* Lexington, Mass.: D. C. Heath and Co., 1971.

Stendhal, Krister. *The Bible and the Role of Women: A Case Study in Hermeneutics.* Philadelphia: Fortress Press, 1966.

Tillich, Paul. *The New Being.* New York: Charles Scribner's Sons, 1955.

Tournier, Paul. *The Whole Person in a Broken World.* New York: Harper & Row, Publishers, 1964.

VonRad, Gerhard. *Genesis.* London: SCM Press Ltd., 1961.

Watts, Alan. *Nature, Man and Woman.* New York: Vintage Books, 1958, 1970.

Yoder, John Howard. *The Politics of Jesus.* Grand Rapids: William B. Eerdmans, 1972.

Articles

Auerbach, Alexander. "Women Sue Insurance Companies." Fort Wayne, Indiana, *News-Sentinel,* February 9, 1974.

Barta, Russell. "Demythologizing Theology." *America,* February 5, 1972, pp. 118-121.

Boynton, Barbara "James Prescott: Touching." *Intellectual Digest,* March 1974, p. 6ff.

Bunch-Weeks, Charlotte. "Women's Oppression: An Overview." *Social Action,* April 1971, pp. 8-17.

Collins, Sheila. "Toward a Feminist Theology." *Christian Century,* August 2, 1972, pp. 796-799.

Cottle, Thomas J. "A Middle American Marriage." *Harper's Magazine,* February 1973, p. 56ff.

Couch, Beatriz Melano. "A Key to the Understanding of the New Humanity." *Church and Society,* September-October 1972, pp. 42-49.

Daly, Mary. "After the Death of God the Father." *Commonweal,* March 12, 1971, pp. 7-11.

Elshtain, Jean Bethke. "Beyond Sexual Politics." *Commonweal,* April 28, 1972, pp. 192-194.

"Father God, Mother Eve." *Time,* March 20, 1972, pp. 58 & 63.

Freud, Sigmund. "Anatomy Is Destiny." *Masculine/Feminine,* edited by Betty Roszak and Theodore Roszak. New York: Harper & Row, 1969, pp. 19-29.

Gordis, Robert. "The Knowledge of Good and Evil in the Old Testament and Qumran Scrolls." *Journal of Biblical Literature,* LXXVI, part II, June 1957, pp. 123-138.

Heide, Wilma Scott. "Sexism Is Dangerous to Your Spiritual Health." *Church and Society,* September-October 1972, pp. 5-8.

Keen, Sam. "Man & Myth: A Conversation With Joseph Campbell." *Psychology Today,* July 1971, p. 35ff.

Kepler, Patricia Budd. "We Need a New Theology." *Church and Society,* September-October 1972, pp. 9-15.

Marvin, Jane Krauss. "Why Do We Resist Liberation?" *Church and Society,* September-October 1972, pp. 16-21.

Miller, Casey, and Swift, Kate, "One Small Step for Genkind." *New York Times Magazine,* April 16, 1972, p. 36ff.

Murray, Pauli. "The Problems of Black Women." *Social Action,* April 1971, pp. 18-21.

Novak, Michael. "Feminine-Masculine Theology." *Commonweal,* June 2, 1972, pp. 302-319.

Palmer, Paul E. "Christian Breakthrough in Women's Lib." *America,* June 19, 1971, pp. 634-637.

Ratagick, Marie. "Two American Welfare Mothers." *Ms.*, June 1973, pp. 74-77.

Reuther, Rosemary. "The Cult of True Womanhood." *Commonweal*, November 9, 1973, pp. 127-132.

_____. "Mother Earth and the Megamachine." *Christianity and Crisis*, December 13, 1971, pp. 267-272.

_____. "Theology by Sex." *The New Republic*, November 10, 1973, pp. 24-26.

Scroggs, Robin. "Paul and the Eschatological Woman." *Journal of the American Academy of Religion*, September 1972, pp. 283-303.

Sontag, Susan. "The Double Standard of Aging." *Saturday Review of the Society*, October 1972, p. 29ff.

Staines, Graham; Jayaratne, Toby Epstein; and Tavris, Carol. "The Queen Bee Syndrome." *Psychology Today*, January 1974, p. 55ff.

Tresemer, David. "Fear of Success; Popular but Unproven" *Psychology Today*, March 1974, pp. 82-85.

Trible, Phyllis. "Depatriarchalizing in Biblical Interpretation." *Journal of the American Academy of Religion*, XLI/1, March 1973, pp. 30-48.

Wedel, Theodore O. "Exposition of Ephesians." *The Interpreter's Bible*, 1953, X:723.

Willis, Ellen. "Economic Realities and the Limits of Feminism." *Ms.*, June 1973, p. 90ff.

Wood, Esther. "Theology Confronts Women's Liberation." *America*, March 13, 1971, pp. 257-259.

Unpublished Material

Talcott, Lou Ann. "Sex Role Stereotyping in the Church of the Brethren Encounter Series for Pre-School Children." Independent research available from Church of the Brethren General Offices.